PRAISE

"A unique perspective on today's world by a former physician and practicing Buddhist nun, beautifully influenced by the wise, gentle, and poetic teachings of Thich Nhat Hanh. A well-curated selection of timeless Buddhist teachings fostering mindful living and conscious dying."

—FRANK OSTASESKI, author of *The Five Invitations*

"Loss and pain can visit us without warning. Sister Dang Nghiem knows this truth of impermanence and shows that compassion, love, and service can emerge through even the deepest suffering. These are tender and intimate teachings revealing that our everyday lives can awaken us to the realization that everything matters—life and death, joy and sorrow, beginnings and endings. A Dharma treasure."

—KOSHIN PALEY ELLISON, author of *Untangled*

"*Live Beautifully, Die Beautifully* has brought me peace from the first moment I started reading Sister Dang Nghiem's words. This book is both human and divine, filled with wisdom and heart. I don't think I will ever stop rereading it."

—BRUCE KASANOFF, executive coach and author of *I Am*

"A profound and moving book of practical wisdom born from a lifetime of living Right Mindfulness. If ever a book was a treasure, this one is; what it offers us is worth more than gems or gold, for it offers us a pathw
I know that I, for one, will be doing my best

—JEREMY DAVID ENG
Democracy and Professor
Penn State University

arrived

at home

in my Body

Live Beautifully, Die Beautifully

FIELD NOTES *from the* EDGE OF IMPERMANENCE

Sister Dang Nghiem, MD

Parallax Press
Berkeley, California

Parallax Press
PO Box 7355
Berkeley, CA 94707
parallax.org

Parallax Press is the publishing division of Plum Village Community of Engaged Buddhism, Inc.

Cover design by Katie Eberle
Interior design by Maureen Forys, Happenstance Type-O-Rama
Cover artwork "Puzzle" © Liliana Buzolin

Printed in the United States of America by Versa Press, Inc.
Printed on FSC-certified paper

Parallax Press's authorized representative in the EU and the EEA is SAS Plum Village at Home - Point UH, 437 Chemin du Pey, Thénac, France
Email: europe@parallax.org

ISBN 978-1-937006-71-6
Ebook ISBN 978-1-967175-37-6

LCCN 2026024369

1 2 3 4 5 VERSA 30 29 28 27 26

FSC
www.fsc.org
MIX
Paper | Supporting responsible forestry
FSC® C005010

In gratitude to Thầy for teaching us how to live beautifully and die beautifully each day. In loving memory of my grandmother, John, Dr. James Doty, Bác Thọ, Em Vũ, Cô Hạnh Quyên, and the many great beings who have blessed me and others with their own courageous and beautiful lives.

—

I would like to be remembered as someone who has the courage to live and to love; someone who is a soulmate to myself and to others; someone who has lived beautifully and died beautifully, smiling into my last breath.

remembering to slow down is not so easy sometimes,
in a world of ambition and so many plans and shiny objects,
but what freedom there is just below the surface of distraction,
like an old reliable friend always present there—ever available,
if we only invest in the moment and have a look that way.

as i walk these days amidst the swirling mass of humanity,
i remember on occasion to have a word with my death,
for my death is with me always; a lifetime companion,
and my death speaks back to me (in not an unfriendly tone),
so it is that we come to an agreement, my death and i,
to meet someday hence upon an open field across the gray river . . .

but i wish not to rush in haste to this appointment,
nay, i prefer to tarry in this world of light and wonder for a while,
for it is here that i have come into acquaintance with a woman so fair,
i have seen her silences and sadness,
for these she does not cloak in shame or guilt,
would that i may spend ten thousand sunsets caressing her hair,
it is she who brings a smile and a song into my world,
i wish to walk the miles with her and spend the nights in her warmth.

for you, my dearest Huong
—john seaver

CONTENTS

FOREWORD

I first became aware of Sister Dang Nghiem in 1997, when I was the associate residency director and chair of our ranking committee at the Contra Costa Regional Medical Center Family Medicine Residency Program in Martinez, California. At that time, she went by her birth name, Huong Huynh, and she was a fourth-year medical student from the University of California, San Francisco (UCSF). She had applied to our residency and been interviewed by our residents and faculty.

I remember fondly when Huong's name came up; our medical team were very excited to talk about her. Not only was she a strong student at one of the most prestigious medical schools in the country, but she and some other medical students had started their own program of visiting and writing letters to inmates in local prisons. Our residency program focused on service to under-resourced communities and we often took care of prisoners in our hospital, yet none of us had ever thought to write letters to these inmates once they left the hospital. We all came to the same conclusion: We must put Huong very high on our list. She was a rare medical student who put service to others above her own need to study for the endless tests and challenges medical students face every day. Huong Huynh, we said, is the real deal, and we wanted her to come join us next year.

So, I was delighted when I saw her name on our list later in March and excited to have her join our residency team the following June. It is easy to say that Huong brought bright energy into whatever space she worked and learned in. She worked hard and learned quickly, and six months into her residency training, she was clearly on her way to becoming a phenomenal physician.

I didn't think much when I noticed she had set up a time to talk with me. When she entered, I was not ready for her news. "Dr. Fish, my boyfriend John recently drowned swimming in the ocean, and I need to take some time off to grieve. I think I need to leave the residency very soon."

Many residents face emotional, social, or family challenges during the rigors of residency training, so I quickly settled into problem-solving mode. "How can we support you? Why don't we make this a three-month leave of absence so we can get you up to speed and not extend your training too much beyond the usual three years?" But Huong did not respond as most first-year residents did. "Dr. Fish, no. I think I must leave. I need to go away, and I don't know if I'm coming back." Understanding the depth of her grief, I agreed to release her from our program. I made it clear she would be welcome back anytime.

A few weeks later, I received a letter from Huong addressed simply to "My dear friends at Martinez." In it she shared that she had found peace and joy at a Buddhist monastery called Plum Village, and she was on her way to becoming a nun. Part of me didn't believe it. How could someone put so much work into getting into one of the greatest medical schools in the world, do so well in medical school, join a very rigorous residency, perform so well—then stop being a doctor altogether? It was inconceivable to me. I continued to send her letters of condolence and support while holding out hope she might return.

A couple of years ago while helping my wife clear some boxes in our garage, I stumbled upon Huong's letter from 1999, just after she left our residency program and joined Plum Village. Reading it again, I could hear the voice of the young physician we had known in Martinez trying to explain the awakening she was experiencing. She wrote eloquently about bringing awareness of her in-breath and out-breath to every step she took at Plum Village, and the comfort and peace that brought her. She described life in community: "We are to be in the present moment, and not pulled away or wrapped up in thoughts of the past or plans and anxiety about the future." She also reflected on how busy our lives had been at Martinez: "After all, we often rush across hallways, answer one pager after another, grab some food quickly on our way to the noon lecture. Where is the time to be aware of our own breathing or our own states of mind?" Then she added a line that stayed with me: "I admit I do not miss being in the world where you are."

At that moment I accepted Huong was not coming back. Rereading her letter many years later, I recognized something else: I still live much of my life in action rather than awareness. Curious about where her path had taken her, I began searching for Huong online. That search led me to her book *Healing: A Woman's Journey from Doctor to Nun*, which I quickly purchased and read. Yes—it was her. Sister Dang Nghiem, MD, writing about her journey from UCSF to Martinez and then to Plum Village after the tragic drowning of her boyfriend, John. Through her story I learned more about her early life, her flight from Vietnam with her brother, and the pain she had carried for many years. I began to understand how the loss of John became the moment that opened a different path for her, the one her grandmother had foretold of becoming a nun.

I've done my fair share of meditation practice and have read many Buddhist teachings about waking up amid suffering. Yet my own awakening has been slower and more incremental than Sister Dang Nghiem's. Becoming a physician, husband, and father has required me to face suffering in many ways. Even now, as I consider what retirement might mean, I find myself moving forward in my usual cautious fashion. By contrast, Huong's transformation—now as Sister Dang Nghiem—remains one of the most courageous acts of awakening I have ever personally witnessed.

Her opening words capture something essential about who Sister Dang Nghiem is:

> *I would like to be remembered as someone who has the courage to live and to love; someone who is a soulmate to myself and to others; someone who has lived beautifully and died beautifully, smiling into my last breath.*

Most of us hope for only the first half of that paradox—to live beautifully. Yet Sister Dang Nghiem invites us to see that living beautifully also means learning how to die beautifully. Life and death arise together from the moment we are born. They are not opposites. Spiritual teachers and scientists alike remind us that our bodies themselves are in a constant process of renewal: older cells dying, new cells being born.

In one of the most moving passages in this book—a letter she wrote after the passing of her beloved teacher Thich Nhat

Hanh—Sister Dang Nghiem reflects on how years of mindful practice allowed her to receive loss without collapsing beneath it. After days of Noble Silence shared by the community, she realized her teacher was not gone. His presence lived on in her breath, in her steps, and in the continuation of the practice. Years earlier, the accumulation of losses in her life had once overwhelmed her. Through deep practice within a loving community, she learned to meet suffering with awareness, steadiness, and compassion.

Sister Dang Nghiem has shown me that who we are and how we live matter far more than any title we hold—doctor, professor, judge, or politician. In truth, she remains both a physician and a Buddhist nun. Her prescriptions may not come in the form of medications, but in mindfulness, compassion, community, and breath. They are teachings that reach the heart and invite us to live more fully and more wisely.

Sister Dang Nghiem's book, like her life, is beautiful. We are blessed that her wisdom has emerged through suffering, practice, and transformation. May you find the peace of beautiful living and dying in the pages that follow.

Namaste,

JEREMY M. FISH, MD
Founding director, John Muir Health Family Medicine Residency Program
February 26, 2026
Walnut Creek, California

INTRODUCTION

The Five Remembrances

On the way to the Ocean of Peace Meditation Hall from my room at Deer Park Monastery in Southern California, where I live, there is a plant with beautiful, rosebud-like flowers. During the first year of the 2020 pandemic, I dried the flowers, pressed them between the pages of books, and used them to make cards. The next year, we received heavy rains, and a major branch broke off in a storm. Only one branch remained, not even as thick as my wrist, now bent low and stripped to the pith at its root. The plant didn't seem salvageable.

Still, I came back the next day with two wooden sticks. I made a tripod and wrapped a wire around the bark to keep it upright. I spoke to the plant, "I don't know if I can save your life or not, but my efforts are a gesture of my gratitude. You bloomed so beautifully last year, and we made many beautiful cards that brought joy and comfort to our lay friends in a time of upheaval. I want you to know I appreciate your life."

Each time I passed on my way back from morning sitting meditation, I watered the plant, touched it, and spoke lovingly to it. At first some leaves turned yellow. Then, they stopped changing color. Just as I was thinking, "Wow, it may survive!" new buds and flowers appeared! Even though it had been injured to its core, with care and the right supportive conditions, the plant healed and flowered. In a quiet way, this small plant and I both learned the same lesson about being hurt and finding the conditions to live on.

I have been a nun in the Plum Village tradition of Engaged Buddhism for more than twenty-five years. To me, Zen teachings and practices are not transcendental or exotic. They are simple: mindful breathing, mindful walking, stopping, deep looking, and attention to what we take in. Our mindfulness shapes what we offer to others. With honest awareness of our thoughts, speech, and actions, we can become a safe refuge for ourselves and those we love. Again and again, I have witnessed that when we attentively care for what is tender in us, peace, healing, and blossoming are possible—even when we were not sure anything could be "salvaged."

Before I came to Plum Village, life had already broken me open many times. Much of my young life was marked by loss and grief. I never knew my father, an American soldier during the war in Vietnam. In 1980, when I was twelve, my mother disappeared. To this day, her body has not been recovered. In 1985, aged seventeen, I came to the United States with my thirteen-year-old brother. I carried with me my grandmother's three wishes: that I would raise my brother well, pursue a higher education, and become a nun. Over the next decade, I worked hard to fulfill her first two wishes. It took many years and two more heart-wrenching deaths before I understood how becoming a nun could serve myself and the world, as my grandmother had foretold. With each loss, the ground beneath me shifted, and yet somehow the life force in me kept pushing me forward.

My brother Sonny and I had to learn English from scratch. One year after we came to the United States, my grandmother—the person who had raised me and taken care of me, a constant foundation of stability in my life both before and after my mother disappeared—died. After finishing high school and college with my newly learned English, I made my way to medical school at UCSF. I wanted to live in a diverse environment where I could learn more than just medicine. In medical school, I had to work especially hard—when I enrolled, I didn't even know what aspirin was. So much common knowledge was new to me.

For years, I applied myself fully to my chosen career. I believed academic success, respectable work, and romantic love would assuage my pain and make up for my losses. Then, when I was thirty-one and had just begun my residency in Family Practice, I lost my partner. John was joyful, peaceful, and deeply spiritual. He was only thirty-three years old when he passed away, but he knew how to live life fully and beautifully. His was the second close death after my emigration, and it woke me up. I looked into my life and asked myself, "If I were to die suddenly, like John did, could I say I had peace, that it was okay to let go?" Sadly, a resounding "No!" arose immediately. Suddenly, the question of a meaningful life was no longer an idea but an urgent, living inquiry.

Three weeks earlier, in August 1999, I had met Zen Master Thich Nhat Hanh for the first time at a mindfulness retreat in Santa Barbara. Meeting "Thầy," as he is affectionately known (*thầy* is Vietnamese for "teacher"), changed the course of my life. Thầy was a monk with a profound practice of mindfulness, which he had forged in the fire of great suffering during the war in Vietnam. In his presence, I tasted for the first time a way of living in which suffering and peace could dwell together, without denying either. After just a few days, I knew he was the spiritual teacher, grandmother, father, mother, and soulmate I had always yearned for.

When John died, I thought of Thầy and of the profound peace and courage that emanated from his gaze and presence. The ferocity of my grief and disillusionment gave me the strength to let go of a career in medicine—of everything I had worked so hard for—to pursue a spiritual life. In the depths of grief, peace was more important to me than anything else. Within three months, I left the hospital and went to Plum Village, Thầy's practice center in southwestern France. Five months later, in May 2000, I was ordained as a nun.

Tragedy taught me that to live beautifully is of the utmost importance, whether we live a long or short life. Devoting my life to understanding and transforming my suffering into safety, compassion, and joy has made it clear how precious this one chance at a human life is. As Einstein wrote, there are two ways to live: as if nothing is a miracle, or as if everything is. If we can spend time with people we love—laughing, holding hands, sharing our joys and our sorrows—it is a blessing. It is a miracle. This miracle is a choice we can learn to make each day. To live beautifully and to die beautifully, moment by moment, is a great gift—not only to ourselves, but to those we love and to the world.

This is the gift that I hope to share with you in these pages. The practices and stories I share arise directly from the discovery that every moment, even the painful ones, can become part of a larger miracle of understanding and love. Like an ant diligently gathering seeds and nectar, I've collected the precious moments of my life with care, hoping to shape them into a shelter for many. You do not need to be a Zen practitioner, or even to think of yourself as a "spiritual" person, to enter this shelter with me; you only need to have a human heart that has known change.

The Five Remembrances, one of the most foundational Zen practices, inspire us to live fully and prepare us for our final moments. Sooner or later, you and I will face our death. The real question is: How have we lived our life? How do we live each moment so our life is beautiful and, when our death arrives, it is beautiful too? The way we live and die, moment by moment, matters. The Five Remembrances have become like a steady bell of mindfulness that calls me back again and again to what truly matters.

In the following pages, I offer my life as a kaleidoscope. Turn it one way, and you'll see the day-to-day; turn it again and you'll see the colors of a humble mindfulness practitioner. Twist it once more and teachings offered directly by the Buddha or by Thầy appear as bright gems. In particular, the Five Remembrances appear again and again in varying forms. We will look at these Remembrances one by one, through each shifting kaleidoscope arrangement, unpacking their lessons and how they can make our lives more precious and meaningful. I hope the beauty of what you see helps you look at your life and our world—grief, despair, and all—with clarity, wisdom, and compassion. My deepest wish is that, as you turn this kaleidoscope, you will also see the colors and patterns of your own life, and discover how much beauty is already there.

Zen teachings begin with four simple observations: There is suffering; suffering has causes; happiness and peace are possible; and there is a path toward them. If these Four Noble Truths are the map, the Five Remembrances are the way the ground feels under our feet. These Remembrances are not abstract truths but living companions: They remind us our lives unfold within conditions no one can escape. We will age—no path avoids growing old. Our bodies will experience sickness, because being alive means being vulnerable. One day we will die; death is not a mistake but part of our nature. Everyone and everything we cherish will change—separation is woven into love itself. And through all of this, our actions continue; they are what remain after our breath has stopped. These five truths can be read slowly, one breath at a time.

1. I am of the nature to grow old. There is no way to escape growing old.
2. I am of the nature to have ill-health. There is no way to escape having ill-health.
3. I am of the nature to die. There is no way to escape death.
4. All that is dear to me and everyone I love are of the nature to change. There is no way to escape being separated from them.
5. Our actions are our true inheritance. Our actions establish the ground on which we stand.

The Five Remembrances turn wisdom teachings into daily practice, into the table we set, the breath we follow, the choices we make. They show us how to live beautifully and, when the time comes, to die beautifully too. Practicing these Remembrances helps us stay grounded and connect more deeply with others, inspiring compassionate actions rooted in knowing the quality of our life and death impacts others. We can live so we benefit our loved ones and the world long after we've taken our last breath. Contemplating the Five Remembrances regularly provides us strength in difficult times. Recognizing our fragility, we cherish what we still have, whatever stage of life we're in—health, youth, relationships, meaningful work—with the capacity to see and to touch beauty.

To contemplate these truths is not to turn away from life, but to turn more fully toward it. The Five Remembrances are not meant to weigh us down, but to invite us to wake up. Each Remembrance invites us to look more deeply into our nature, to understand suffering and joy, and to live with presence and love. Each reveals that impermanence is not our enemy, but our teacher. When we touch the reality that everything changes—our bodies, our health, those we love, what we care about—we discover the freedom to live more deeply and love more honestly. This awareness allows us to care for our life and the lives around us without clinging or fear. When we can stand in the truth of impermanence, even for a few breaths, we find we are less afraid of our own suffering and more able to accompany others in theirs.

I hope the Five Remembrances support you in cultivating clarity and compassion, both for yourself and those you accompany. May you feel encouraged to meet your days, bright or shadowed, with true presence and loving awareness. May we, together, live beautifully and die beautifully, smiling into our last breath. If at any point you feel touched or stirred by what you read, you might simply pause, place a hand on your heart, and breathe. Allow the Five Remembrances to be not just ideas, but a lived experience in your body and mind.

SISTER DANG NGHIEM
April 25, 2026

LIVE BEAUTIFULLY, DIE BEAUTIFULLY—TODAY

If you wish, before we continue, you may pause for a brief guided contemplation of the Five Remembrances.

Sit or stand in a relaxed, upright position. Let your body be supported by the earth beneath you. Allow the breath to settle on its own. Each in-breath is an arrival. Each out-breath is a releasing.

When you feel ready, follow each of the lines below with your own natural breathing.

Breathing in, I am aware that I am of the nature to grow old.

Breathing out, I gently acknowledge the changes in my body and mind.

Breathing in, I am aware that I am of the nature to have ill-health.

Breathing out, I embrace my fears and vulnerabilities with compassion.

Breathing in, I am aware that I am of the nature to die.

Breathing out, I touch the preciousness of this moment.

Breathing in, I give rise to the awareness that I will be separated from all that is dear to me.

Breathing out, I gently loosen my grip on expectations and embrace myself and others with greater acceptance.

Breathing in, I am aware that my actions are my true continuation.

Breathing out, I choose thoughts, words, and deeds rooted in kindness and understanding.

Breathing in, I make the aspiration to live beautifully each day.

Breathing out, I make the aspiration to die beautifully each day.

Take one more gentle breath. When you are ready, open your eyes or simply lift your gaze, carrying this presence forward into whatever comes next.

1

I am of
the nature
to grow old.
There is no
way to escape
growing old.

Growing old is one of the most intimate teachers we will meet. Our body changes, our roles change, and the ways we understand ourselves gradually shift. Yet aging is not only a process of loss. It is also a process of ripening. To grow old is to move into the mystery of time's slow unfolding. In a culture devoted to youth and its illusions of permanence, the First Remembrance draws us toward reverence for the wrinkles earned by weathering love and loss, and the softening of edges that once cut us. Growing old is not what happens to us, but what we become—if we let ourselves. It is an apprenticeship to wisdom, the slow bloom of becoming real. The invitation is simple: to grow old mindfully, with eyes open, palms open, heart open. Aging, like tides and seasons, is not a flaw in life's design.

Cherishing the Body that Ages

This morning, I studied my hands. The skin is looser now, and my veins rise like little rivers. I rubbed in a spoonful of coconut oil and whispered, "I am of the nature to grow old." It wasn't a lament. It was gratitude for everything these hands have carried and let go. Impermanence is not an idea for me; it has already torn through my life in ways that shaped every step I take now. I can see it in my own hands.

Sometimes I still talk to John, who died at thirty-three. "Honey, I am growing old," I tell him, tracing the small constellations along my wrist, the age spots, the wrinkles. I am already twenty-four years older than John ever was, and twenty-one years older than my own mother! To me, this isn't morbid; it's cherishing life as it is, right at this moment.

When I was in college, youth seemed infinite. A classmate of mine—a freshman from a small town—spent hours sunbathing in her bikini on the dorm lawn, her skin turning darker each week. On weekends she'd head to parties that often lasted until morning, filled with music, laughter, and the thrill of being free for the first time. She was bright and full of potential, but somewhere between late nights and missed classes, she began to fall behind. By sophomore year, she'd lost her scholarship and left school. I didn't understand then how fragile our energy is, how easily it's squandered.

Looking back, I'm grateful I didn't lose myself in the same ways. I was still adjusting to life in the US, struggling to learn English and keep up with my studies. Yet I carried my own illusions of invincibility. In Vietnam, light skin was prized, yet in Arizona I refused to wear hats in the sun. I had five fancy hats, but I only wore them at night, dancing under disco lights.

It wasn't until I became a nun that I gradually learned to cherish my body, my youth, and my life energy. However old we are, this is the youngest we will ever be. So, let us celebrate our bodies: Care for them, enjoy them, and remember that they, too, will pass. I don't want to outwit aging; I want to befriend it. Each day, I practice loosening my grip—on hurry, on performance, on the face I used to know. I am learning to live in a body that tells the truth.

If you wish, you can explore this tenderness in your own body. Find a quiet place to sit, lie down, or stand. Let your breath settle. Feel the body that has carried you—its weight, its warmth, its quiet pulse of life. If you like, you can slowly read the following lines while staying connected to your breath.

Breathing in, I recognize parts of my body that have changed with time.
Breathing out, I smile with these changes.

Breathing in, I whisper to my body, "You have been kind to me and served me well."
Breathing out, I whisper, "Thank you."

Breathing in, I remember that I am of the nature to grow old.
Breathing out, I touch tenderness for this body and for this life.

Breathing in, I feel the strength of those who have aged before me.
Breathing out, I feel their calm and presence in me.

Breathing in, I touch the dreams that still nourish me.
Breathing out, I release what no longer serves.

Breathing in, I aspire to live beautifully—cherishing what is here.
Breathing out, I aspire to die beautifully—releasing fear and regret in every moment.

Sit quietly for a few more breaths, feeling the body breathing itself. Nothing is missing. Nothing is wasted. There is only change, unfolding.

Intention as Nutriment

The Buddha spoke of four kinds of nutriments. The first is edible food. The second is sensory impressions—what we take in through our eyes, ears, nose, tongue, skin, and mind. The third is volition or intention, the dreams and aspirations that give our life direction. Just as the body needs food, the mind needs purpose to feel alive and to thrive. The fourth is consciousness itself—the body-mind needs consciousness to live.

I once felt romantically drawn to a fellow monk, and the feeling was mutual. One day, half-jokingly, he said, "We could leave monastic life together. I'll take care of you and make sure you always have plenty of vegetables." I laughed and said, "But I don't only need vegetables." Something in that exchange jolted me awake and reminded me of my deep aspiration to be free from suffering. I saw clearly enough to let go of the infatuation I had been harboring.

Our dreams and aspirations give us direction, but it's important to ask: Where do they come from? Do they help us know ourselves more deeply each day, or do they distract us from who we are? Are they rooted in what we truly want to do and contribute to the world? Or have we borrowed them—from family, from society, from the babble around us? It's worth pausing to feel the current beneath our dreams and aspirations, to sense the true intention that carries them.

We spend so much energy and time running away from what is here. We have this notion that youth is beauty and old age is ugliness, undesirable, frightening. These ideas are especially strong in our modern culture. In the past, elders were honored for their wisdom and experience. Today, we often prize technology and novelty instead. It can leave us feeling outdated, easily replaced. It's natural to have fears, and we sometimes even try to hide them from ourselves and others. Yet, wherever we go, there we are.

Instead of feeling frightened or ashamed of wrinkles and age spots, see them as the marks of your life—the love you've given and received, the support, the memories, the many seasons you have lived. When I look at my eyes, I see my mother's eyes. As I age, I see more of my grandmother there, too. I've learned to cherish the experiences that have shaped me. Do we truly want to erase all of this? The key is not to remain young or to reclaim what we once had. It is to cherish what we still have right now, to realize interconnection in daily life as a deep intention, and to be at peace with where we are. In this way, we welcome everything. Old age can be dignified and beautiful.

Unconscious Influences

This morning at breakfast, Ari and his parents sat across from me at the table. His mother had been on staff at the Teens Camp in Deer Park while she was pregnant with him. Now he's already two and a half—so chubby and active, with a little ponytail of blond, curly hair.

At one point, Ari picked up a small bunch of grapes still attached to the stem. He put one grape in his mouth, but the others and the stem got in the way, and he froze for a moment, unsure of what to do. I gestured with both hands, showing him how to pull the grape from the stem. He watched me intently, then mimicked the movement—and it worked! He did it again. Then, once more, he tried to eat a grape still on the stem, realized it wasn't so easy, and pulled it off. From that point on, he became an expert grape-detacher.

It struck me—I taught Ari a skill today, one he'll carry into countless small moments: pulling the cap off a pen, a knife from its sheath, who knows what else. He'll never consciously remember, "Sister D taught me this skill on April 24, 2025." It will just become a natural, instinctive part of him, as if he always knew how to do it.

My brother Sonny once told me he learned to smoke from an older girl—someone I'd had as a classmate in my English as a Second Language (ESL) class. When he was in ninth grade, she barely glanced his way. By tenth grade, he'd grown so tall and handsome that she started hanging around. One day while they were together, she asked, "You know how to blow circles with a cigarette?" That was his first puff. He wanted to look cool for her. Since then, he's been a one-pack-a-day smoker. He has tried to quit before, but it has never really stuck.

Isn't that how most things are? Movements, habits, views, ways of being—we've absorbed them from our parents, siblings, teachers, the people around us. For better or worse, they become part of who we are and of what we share. We, too, constantly transmit something through our words, our presence, even our smallest actions. They ripple out into others' lives, shaping them. Are we aware of our influences? Do we take responsibility for them?

Our faces and names may not be remembered, but our actions might echo in someone's life for years to come, nurturing or harming them without us even knowing. Being aware of our influence on others is part of the wisdom—the gift—of being of the nature to grow old.

Staying Young

People often notice that monks and nuns appear ten to twenty years younger than they are. When Thầy was alive, no one could guess his age. Each year he seemed more radiant, more at ease. The secret isn't a special diet or miracle cream: It's learning to approach life with calmness and equanimity.

When we're not mindful, our attention is somewhere else. Something falls, and we startle. When mindfulness is present—when mind and body are connected, aware of what is going on in this moment—we respond differently. The same thing may fall, but we remain centered. There's no panic, no jolt. We don't cringe or frown as much. We meet each moment as it is. Our mind doesn't need to "fly back from the past, from the future, or from another continent," as Thầy often said, to catch up with what just happened. It's already here, ready to receive the moment.

The Chinese character for mindfulness (念) combines two parts: "now" (今) and "mind" (心). This character also means "to remember." Often, our mind is lost in the past or in the future—in projects or in dreams, in what is gone or not yet come. We are not present to experience what is happening. We try to turn away from our bodies getting old, from the subtle or obvious changes that remind us of our mortality. When our mind is here and now, it remembers and can be with what is true, what is real.

Scientific studies of monks and nuns who meditate have shown measurable differences in brain activities and cortisol levels. Stress takes a toll. It weakens the immune system, clouds our ability to respond with clarity, and makes it harder to endure hardship. Stress ages us quickly; it can, after all, turn our hair white overnight. When my partner passed away, I saw new long strands of white hair on my head the very next morning. I was only thirty-one.

With steady mindfulness, stress still arises, but it doesn't register in the body as a threat. Mindfulness keeps the body from slipping into traumatic, reactive states that drain our vitality. With age, some people become hypersensitive, rigid, cranky, bitter, or forgetful. When we take life too seriously, we get trapped. We lose sight of meaning. When we live a life of practice, we age differently. I've seen it in Thầy and in many of my elders—they become more joyful, lighter, and more childlike as time passes. Aging often makes it easier to laugh and appreciate the humor and delight in everyday life, as what truly matters—and what lies within our control—comes into clearer focus. Mindfulness lets us hold things lightly and stay fresh so we can approach life spaciously.

At a recent retreat, I hugged an older person. I felt her body soften and heard a deep sigh of release as we embraced. Afterward she told me, "Nobody has hugged me for a long time. People don't like to hug an old person."

It is true that babies carry the sweetness of fresh breath, while the elderly, the sick, and the dying may bear the scent of decay. All the more reason for friends and loved ones to continue to offer mindful touch and affection, no matter how old or young someone looks.

LIVE BEAUTIFULLY, DIE BEAUTIFULLY—TODAY

Checking In

Let's check in with our feelings. Take a deep breath and become aware of the emotions present within you. Notice whether they are pleasant, neutral, mixed, or unpleasant. Say to yourself and your emotions, "I'm here for you. Help me not to drown in you or run away from you." Check in with whatever arises, whether it's craving, anxiety, sorrow, or anything else, and take a few breaths to simply be with it.

Where do you feel the emotion in your body? Is it in your chest, abdomen, or hands? Gently breathe into these areas and smile. As you exhale, smile softly and allow the breath to help you relax and release any physical or emotional tension you may be holding.

Five Sensual Desires

In Buddhism, there are five kinds of sensual pleasure or desires. The first is pleasure derived from wealth or money; the second from attractive forms and sex; the third from fame or celebrity; the fourth from overeating; and the fifth from oversleeping or seeking comfort as escape. The desire for sensual pleasures tends to be strongest when we are young, when time still feels unlimited and we believe satisfaction will come from having "more." As we age, our desires often shift, shaped by our habits, experiences, and the growing awareness that our time is not endless.

Screen-driven stimulation is widespread and normalized in modern society. Whether on public transportation, at a restaurant, in a social gathering, or at home, nearly everyone is glued to a screen. Children are often pacified by iPads, while teens turn to games and movies to escape or manage unpleasant emotions rather than learning how to care for them. We've become accustomed to short dopamine rushes, losing touch with who we are, where we are, or even what day it is. We are disconnected from our own bodies, and from the person right in front of us. With mindfulness, we see how easily we trade the present moment for distraction, and how precious our attention truly is.

Often, we mistake sense pleasure for true happiness. Sense pleasure depends on stimulation—something pleasant to see, taste, hear, or experience. When the stimulation fades, the pleasure fades as well, and we begin searching for the next experience. In this way, desire easily pulls us from one moment to another, always looking for something more. Often, we believe happiness lies either in more stimulation or some future moment when everything will finally come together. We chase pleasure now, or we postpone happiness for later—after the next achievement, the next promotion, the next stage of life. But both habits keep us from touching the peace already available in the present moment.

True happiness is different. It does not depend on constant stimulation or future achievements. In walking meditation, the practice of aligning our steps with our breath as we turn our awareness toward the sensation of our feet touching the earth, we experience lightness and peace in our body and mind. We touch happiness directly in every moment, not as a delayed reward once we get better at walking, become someone else, or achieve something else. Some people, after having obtained a degree, are still unhappy, so they relentlessly pursue another qualification. They may end up with three or four degrees without ever touching true contentment.

In one case, a woman recounted that her husband always promised her that they would travel extensively after he retired. On the very first day of his retirement, she found him dead in the garage from a heart attack. All their dreams had been postponed for years, only to be completely shattered in one instant. Aging teaches us not to postpone our life, not to wait for later to be truly present for ourselves and for those we love.

The beauty industry often preys upon our insecurities, promising that lotions and potions will make us younger, prettier, and thus happier. This too reflects our sensual desire for attractive forms—the wish to preserve youth and beauty so we may feel more loved or valued. Yet mindful breathing and relaxation can nourish our body far more deeply than any expensive cream. As we grow older, we may discover that caring for the body begins not with cosmetics but with the way we breathe, smile, relax, and inhabit each moment.

Let us take a moment to touch joy, peace, and happiness right in our breathing, right now. Smile to your in-breaths. Relax into your out-breaths. This is something you can practice at home at any moment. You can practice while you are reading this book, too.

Most of us carry cell phones with us throughout the day. Each notification promises a small burst of stimulation—a message, an image, a piece of news, or a moment of recognition. We may feel compelled to check it immediately. Yet each ring or vibration can also trigger a subtle—or not so subtle—stress response in our body. Our breath might stop or speed up, our heart beats faster, and our muscles tense. Over time, these repeated reactions exhaust our nervous system, leaving us irritable and fatigued—not as a result of time itself, but because of how we live it. Instead of immediately reaching for our phone, we can use the sound as a bell of mindfulness. When the phone rings, we can pause for one in-breath and one out-breath, smiling and relaxing our face. If we truly care for ourselves, we might take a second breath, or even a third. In this way, something that normally feeds distraction becomes an opportunity to return to the present moment.

Seeing Through Desire

Desire is one of our most familiar teachers. From the moment we open our eyes in the morning, we are drawn toward what pleases and away from what disturbs. The Buddha understood this thoroughly. He saw that we become enamored with form because form is pleasurable—our eyes delight in color and shape, our ears in melody, our minds in praise and approval. It is not wrong to enjoy these things. The danger comes when we mistake them for lasting, when we cling to them as though they can complete us.

We fall in love with the curve of a shoulder, the timbre of a voice, the warmth of a hand. These are moments of delight, but they are also invitations to look more deeply. When we chase after desire or pleasure without awareness, our joy becomes a trap. We begin to live for stimulation rather than connection, and we lose our freedom. The Buddha called this being "captivated by form."[1] It is not a moral failing, but simply the nature of an untrained mind to seek what feels good and flee what feels painful.

Yet the untrained mind has the capacity to awaken. The reality that life is not only pleasure but also sorrow, not only sweetness but also bitterness, offers us the chance to see through appearances. If everything were only delightful, we would never question our attachment. It is precisely because we age, because the body falters, because what we love changes or disappears that liberation is possible. Pain, in this way, is not a dead end but an opening.

In our youth, we may spend vast amounts of energy chasing beauty and sensation—hours in front of mirrors or screens, endlessly measuring ourselves against others. Our body, feelings, and thoughts are not possessions, though. They are gifts of the universe, on loan for a short while. When we see clearly, we stop trying to grasp them and begin to care for them with more equanimity—a profound gift to ourselves and to the world.

Impermanence is not an abstract idea. It reveals itself through every ache, every gray hair, every change in the seasons of our skin. Once, a young man sent me a poem praising my glowing skin and strawberry-shaped lips. The very next day, I accidentally wet my pants while sitting on my bed—completely unprecedented, without warning or control! I was stunned for a moment. Then my first thought was, "Thank you for keeping me humble!" Instead of shame, I felt compassion for this aging body, which had served me faithfully for so long. That small, humbling moment was a perfect Zen stick that struck me and woke me up from my reverie. The immediate compassion and acceptance for my body's fragility was the fruit of my practice with the Five Remembrances. I tore up the poem and felt strangely free.

Awareness of impermanence sobers the heart. When we look deeply at the body—our own or another's—we see its beauty and its trembling fragility. The same hands that reach out in love today will one day loosen their grip. The same voice that sings with joy will one day fall quiet. Seeing this, we no longer love to possess; we love to honor. Gratitude replaces grasping.

This, too, is the practice: to breathe with what comes and goes, to let every joy and sorrow pass through like clouds across the sky. When we see the fleeting nature of desire, it loses its power to bind us. We can savor what is pleasant without clutching it, and stay steady through what is painful without resistance. This is the middle way—not denial or indulgence, but intimacy with the real, breath by breath.

We can practice this humility every day by simply observing what the body releases. In the Buddha's time, monastics trained to release attachment and craving for the body by visiting charnel grounds to contemplate the nine stages of a corpse's decomposition. I've adapted this practice in a gentler, more accessible form: I make a point of looking into the toilet bowl before I flush. The color, consistency, odor, and amount of excrement I produce imprints itself on my mind, a reminder that the same body we admire, crave, and try to perfect is also quietly engaged in the ordinary work of digestion, transformation, and release.

The Buddha once told a goddess who struggled with desire, "When you see the true nature of desire, the desiring mind will not be born."[2] To see desire's nature is to see that it is empty of all stability or permanence—it appears, burns brightly, and fades like a flame in wind. When we recognize this pattern, we can greet it gently: "Hello, craving. Hello, wanting." We smile, we breathe, and in that instant, we taste freedom.

No one can tempt us more than we tempt ourselves. And no one can liberate us but ourselves. Realizing this, the tempter and the tempted gradually become more free.

Beautiful Eyes

Attachment can also arise among monastics. In one instance, the brother and sister involved were lovely and wonderful people. They were kind and hardworking, taking care of the Sangha to the best of their abilities. I could understand perfectly how they might fall in love.

One day, I asked my sister, "What do you like about him?"

She replied innocently, "I like his eyes."

Indeed, that brother's eyes were beautiful and mesmerizing. Knowing that my sister had become a nun when she was a young teenager with little worldly experience, I replied, "Do you know that if you leave with him, it won't be only his eyes you'll be looking at? You'll have to look at his body, too."

My sister blushed crimson and replied, "No! I don't think about that."

"Well, my dear," I said, "you'd better."

I told her this brother had carried a great deal of suffering when he first came to the practice. He was morbidly obese and severely depressed. Within one year of practice, he lost over a hundred pounds and looked so bright and healthy, I hardly recognized him. I explained to my sister that his transformation relied on both the practice and the supportive community. If he were to disrobe and return to lay life, the stress could lead to his becoming depressed and unhealthy once more.

My sister seemed unfazed by this, so I went to the office and searched online for an image of a nude man with an obese body to help my sister confront the reality of what stress can do to a body. I was nervous the whole time—anyone could walk into the office. What would they think if they saw what Sister D was looking at? In any case, I had to search for quite a while.

In the end, I found an image, printed it out, and gave it to my sister.

"Look at this picture, my dear younger sister," I told her. "This is what our brother might look like if he were stressed and unhappy."

She was so embarrassed she refused to look at the image in front of me, so I left it on the table. I don't know whether she looked at it or not, but I had done my best to help my sister understand that neither falling in love with a person's beautiful form nor the feeling of love itself is likely to last without nurturing and supportive conditions. I also hoped that if she truly wanted to be with him, she would accept him as he is—emotionally and physically, in whatever state he may be in. In the end, he disrobed while she remained a nun.

How the Mind Sees

In the Zen tradition, language is more than a vessel for meaning; it is a landscape of insight. The Dharma has traveled for thousands of years on the back of Chinese characters—old symbols that do not merely say something, but show it. These characters can profoundly illustrate how words hold meaning, often carrying within their forms the very spirit of what they name. For example, in many classical characters, a subtle "heart" element is tucked beneath the surface of the form, reminding us that perception always involves both the senses and the heart-mind.

In Buddhist psychology, perception is not simply what the eye sees, but how the mind interprets what is seen. *Sense consciousness* enables a sign or appearance to be perceived as it is, while *store consciousness* catalogs experiences, compares them with new input, forms perceptions, and passes judgments. For example, when a sense organ such as the eye is in contact with a sense object such as a tree, sense consciousness perceives an image of a tree. This image is then processed in the store consciousness, which gives rise to a perception such as, "That's a nice tree!" or "That tree could damage the house!" It is not solely the external object but also the mind that generates perceptions and gives rise to attitudes, feelings, and reactions of attraction or aversion. Therefore, perception is not only what the eye sees, but how the mind interprets what is seen. Wherever there is perception, there is often misperception and deception.

The Chinese character for perception (想) reflects this understanding: The upper components represent the tree and the eye, while the lower part symbolizes the mind. In other words, what we see is always shaped by the mind that interprets it. Mindful breathing trains us to simply recognize the in-breaths and out-breaths as they are, without adding more thoughts to them. It is a way of clearing the mind and allowing spaciousness that makes it possible to see without perceiving. When our mind can remain calm and still, past experiences will not interfere when we see a person in front of us, whether they are known or unknown to us. Otherwise, the moment someone walks in, a thought may arise: "I dislike that person. Our last encounter (whether last week or years ago) was terrible."

Almost instantly, our mind shuts down and shuts out the person, making us unable to see the person in the present moment. Or, if they resemble another person who caused us suffering, we may still discriminate against them. Likewise, if someone reminds us of a pleasant experience, we feel the impulse to draw close to them. A woman once shared with me that when she met her husband, she felt an immediate sense of familiarity. Only after they got married did she realize what felt familiar was his emotional absence, because her parents had been the same way throughout her life!

Indeed, perception plays a fundamental role in most romantic relationships. In the beginning, we hardly know our new partner—we are attracted to their form, through sight, sound, smell, touch, and assumptions. With time, we discover how our partner inevitably differs from what we have imagined. When our perceptions cloud our vision and we can't reconcile them with the reality that reveals itself, relationships can easily fall into disillusionment, disappointment, and the loss of respect and dignity. Our habit of adding perceptions means that attachment inevitably goes in tandem with aversion—the very form that once seduced us, we now no longer want to look at. Have you ever experienced this change of heart? It's actually a change of perception.

Whenever perceptions arise, breathe! Calm them, see them, and hear them clearly so you are not swept away by them. Mindfulness practice and working with the Five Remembrances help us garner more equanimity so we can see things clearly, as they are. When we can see clearly, not adding anything, we are free.

Nature of Non-Self

The First Remembrance teaches us we are of the nature to age and grow old. As we observe the body changing year by year—hair graying, skin softening, strength rising and falling—we begin to see that what we call "self" is not fixed or permanent. Aging reveals the truth of non-self: This body and mind are processes in constant transformation, rather than something solid we can possess or control.

When we do not see the truth of non-self, we easily fall into comparison. The Buddha taught that as long as we see ourselves as greater, lesser, or even equal to others, our mind cannot be at peace:

> *If you think you are greater, less than, or equal, you cause dissension.*
>
> *When those three complexes have ended, nothing can agitate your mind.*[3]

Wrong views about permanence and a separate self arise simultaneously. Impermanence reveals the movement of all things in time; non-self shows their boundless connection in space. Graphically speaking, impermanence is on the X-axis of time, and non-self is on the Y-axis of space. Aging is one of the clearest expressions of impermanence. When we see how the body continuously changes through time, our belief in a separate and unchanging self loosens.

"If you think you are greater, less than, or equal, you cause dissension." In Vietnamese, the word "dissension" carries a deeper sense of chaos and entanglement than the English synonyms "division" or "conflict" might. The three complexes of inferiority, superiority, and equality result in entanglement and cause chaos in thoughts, feelings, and attitudes as well as speech and action. We discriminate against this person or that group of people. We grasp another person, other identity, or other issue. We are divided from within. We are divided as a family, as a nation, as a world—all because of the wrong perception that we are a separate self. "This is who I am." "I am only this, not that." This sense of separation is the self, the ego talking, and it is the basis for much suffering.

Some people wonder how "equality" could lead to suffering, thinking that equality is noble. Equality is a complex of the ego because it rests on comparison, on seeing ourselves as separate from others, even if doing so leads to a claim of sameness. Even equality keeps the idea of "us" and "them" alive.

The insight of *interbeing*—the interconnected, interdependent nature of everything—is the antidote to our wrong perceptions of a fixed, separate, immutable self. It is the living expression of impermanence and non-self: "This is in that, and that is in this." "This is because that is." "This is not because that is not." In interbeing, we see how much is in the "I" and the "me": mother, father, human ancestors, land ancestors, animal ancestors, plant ancestors, even mineral ancestors are essential to our existence.

Thầy often reminded us not to be content with transforming only small sufferings: "Practice for true love and true freedom!" Indeed, the transformation of the three complexes—superiority, inferiority, and equality—leads to true love and true freedom. In the light of interbeing, the insight of the interconnectedness of all things, we learn to protect not only ourselves but also animals, plants, and minerals, as well as other peoples and nations. We see we are inseparable, intricately connected, dependent on each other. Wrong perceptions fall away, and we find ourselves unlimited and whole within the great web of life.

You Think So?

As we age, our perceptions of ourselves and the world can become especially rigid if we are not mindful. When our sense of self becomes solid and fixed, our perceptions do too. Thầy often encouraged us to look again, to check our certainty, to question even the views we hold dearest. Aging itself is natural. Much of the suffering around aging comes from our perceptions of it.

Yet these insights around growing older don't always translate into daily life without practice. Thầy would write calligraphy—simple phrases meant to be companions in practice—to remind us to come back to our presence and to question our habitual views. One day, as Thầy sat nearby creating one calligraphy after another, he looked up and asked, "Do you want Thầy to write one for you?" I was so happy that Thầy could read my mind. I asked him to write: "You think so?" This simple question is dear and close to my heart, and it has become a lifelong practice; perhaps it may help you as well.

There is humor and lightness in these three words. When a strong view or emotion arises, "You think so?" becomes a breath-wide space between impulse and reaction, revealing how much the mind clings to "me" and "mine." This practice isn't about fostering insecurity, but about noticing how our habitual views and fears shape what we see and do.

In Zen, we have a saying: "Great doubt, great enlightenment." Great doubt is not anxiety, but openness—a spacious questioning that lets us see through the illusion of a fixed self. When doubts arise from unresolved suffering, insecurity, or bias, we see through lenses of fear and repeat the same inner narratives again and again, mistaking them for truth. Great doubt—the kind that leads to insight—arises when we ask "You think so?" with spaciousness rather than fear. When we meet our own assumptions with "You think so?" the mind becomes quieter and more receptive. We can see what is happening without egoic coloring—the very heart of non-self.

This practice of inquiry reflects a central Zen insight about perception: Our view of the world shapes our lived reality. "You think so?" helps us notice how fixed views solidify our sense of identity and may separate us from others.

When perception is habitual, we automatically interpret the world through fear or preference. "You think so?" pauses that automaticity. It becomes a door of ease instead of confusion, a moment where we ask not "What do I think?" but "Why do I think so?"

Mindful inquiry is a way to meet experience directly, before judgment and interpretation take over. When we practice "You think so?" with honesty and kindness, we bring spaciousness to our perception. We are no longer trapped in reaction, becoming open to surprise, presence, and connection.

Doors of Perception

There are two beautiful Chinese characters that illustrate the practice of mindful inquiry. They both depict doors. In one character, a moon sits between two doors (閒). This character means *ease*. In another character, there is a market between two doors (鬧). This character means *chaos*.

We have many doors: the two doors of the eyes, the two doors of the ears, and the doors of the nose, the mouth, the body, the skin, and the mind. The mind itself is a wide-open door.

The question is: Do we place the moon at these doors, or do we place the market? Input affects output, and vice versa. What we consume shapes how we see the world and how we live our lives. The quality of our life depends on how we guard these doors. Doors are not only for opening; they are also for closing. We practice opening and closing them mindfully to protect our body and mind, to invite ease rather than chaos, clarity rather than confusion. In a world of constant input and subtle conditioning, caring for our doors requires effort and intention.

According to Dr. James Doty, 99.99995 percent of information enters our senses without conscious awareness.[4] Yet this unconscious input still shapes our thoughts, emotions, speech, and actions. That is why mindful consumption and choosing a supportive environment are essential practices for a peaceful, happy life.

Distorted perception often shows itself most clearly in the way we see our bodies. A woman who is vibrant and healthy may look in the mirror and see only what she believes is wrong—too big, too soft, too different. Men also suffer from body dysmorphia; muscle dysmorphia, sometimes called "bigorexia," leads many boys and men to feel they're not muscular enough, no matter how strong they become. These are examples of perception becoming tyranny.

This distortion does not end with youth. In fact, aging often magnifies these perceptions, as we compare our changing bodies with the cultural ideals of youth. As we age, we often carry these misperceptions with us, fearing wrinkles, sagging skin, a softening body. We see our aging face and forget the life it carries. We see our changed body and forget its strength, its survival. We forget to love what has endured.

Our brain is a predicting machine. It constantly anticipates and categorizes. This can be useful, but it can also cause suffering when we mistake predictions for reality. Mindful breathing allows us to meet experience directly, before judgment and interpretation arise.

Thầy spoke of three doors of ease—emptiness, non-perception, and non-expectation—which quietly underlie this practice. The mind, untrained, mistakes the surface for the whole. It mistakes a shadow for a story. That is why non-perception is such a powerful door. It allows us to stop, to breathe, and to gently ask ourselves, "You think so?"

A way of understanding emptiness is through *interbeing.* Sometimes it's enough to notice: *I am not separate. My body contains my mother, my father, the earth, and the breath of every being that has ever lived.* This is the first door of ease.

The second door—*non-perception*—reminds us not to believe everything we think. To practice non-perception is to pause and ask, "You think so?" when a story arises—about ourselves, about someone else, about the world. Not to reject it, but to gently release our grip. This is especially tender and necessary as we age, when perceptions shaped by comparison, memory, and cultural ideals can become rigid and unforgiving.

When we practice signlessness, not mistaking a label for the thing itself, we see our judgments arise and gently ask, "You think so?" We breathe, smile, and create space. We learn to meet people and situations with freshness rather than habit. This helps us bring the moon to our doors instead of the market. It allows ease and spaciousness to arise in our lives, moment by moment.

The third door of ease and spaciousness is aimlessness, which Thầy also described as *non-expectation*. In fact, non-expectation naturally follows non-perception. When we have a perception, we also have anticipation, and from anticipation comes expectation. I give you something so you give something back to me. I love you so you will love me back.

This is how we end up perpetually disappointed. When things turn out as we expect, we take them for granted. When they don't, we feel disappointed or distressed. Most of the time, things turn out differently anyway, because there are so many conditions involved that we cannot possibly anticipate them all. This can feel especially painful as we age, when life no longer follows the timelines we once imagined for our bodies, our relationships, or our lives. The practice of interbeing and of non-perception helps us touch non-expectation. We learn simply to do something for the joy of doing it.

For example, lately I've been spending time learning Chinese characters. I sometimes ask myself, "Sister D, why are you learning this? It takes so much effort. If you stop for a month, you'll probably forget everything. What are you going to do with all this?" I smile and answer myself, "I'm just grateful I can still learn. I'm grateful I have the time and space. I learn simply for the joy of learning."

Just like this, you care for someone because you cherish them, because you are able to care for them—not because they will give you something back. That is non-expectation, and it is deeply liberating.

These three doors—emptiness, non-perception, and non-expectation—are doors to ease that we can practice in our daily lives. In this way, even as the body changes with age, the mind can remain open, fresh, and free.

LIVE BEAUTIFULLY, DIE BEAUTIFULLY— TODAY

Touching Nirvana

Before we try to change anything about aging or desire, we begin by learning how to sit with what is already here. We don't have to wait for a great loss or a dramatic turning point to begin letting go. We can begin now, gently allowing the body and mind to show us what we are holding.

In our own practice, we can learn to touch the coolness of Nirvana every day. Each time we notice a craving arising, we can breathe with it instead of feeding it. This is like pouring a little water on the fire. Each time we release a grudge, let go of an expectation, or soften a judgment, we cool the mind. Over time, the fever of grasping subsides. What remains is quiet joy, clarity, acceptance, and love.

Even as our bodies grow frail or disfigured with age or illness, we can smile with peace in our hearts. Venerable Giác Thanh, the former abbot of Deer Park Monastery, wrote before his death:

Skin and flesh are decomposing,
this body is withering.
Yet my spirit is still joyful like spring flowers.
Mountains and rivers are great,
so, no fear for this tiny body.
I'm returning it
to the immense earth and sky.

Sitting quietly with the breath, letting awareness nourish our body just as sunlight nourishes a flower, is a simple way to touch Nirvana. When we breathe without trying to change anything, we can notice how tension, insecurity, and frustration rise and fall on their own. The more gently we look, the more we soften.

From the gentle observation of mere recognition, even the unpleasant becomes a doorway into joy and stability. Peace is revealed beneath waves of emotion like still water beneath a stirred surface. You can explore this in your own body, right now, with the breath as your guide. Read or speak the following lines to yourself as you follow your breath, applying one line to each of your inhales and exhales:

Breathing in, I am aware of my in-breath, as it is.
Breathing out, I am aware of my out-breath, as it is.

Breathing in, I feel my body.
Breathing out, I smile to my body.

Breathing in, I notice where it hurts or tightens.
Breathing out, I soften around it.

Breathing in, I notice a difficult feeling.
Breathing out, I hold it with care.

Breathing in, I notice my capacity to be here.
Breathing out, I smile to that capacity.

When we meet ourselves gently, aging becomes a deepening rather than a decline.

More Than a Name

A childhood classmate recently came to Deer Park Monastery to visit me. We had attended the same school in Vietnam for many years, though we did not really know each other then. She was part of a group called "the Four Mischiefs," while I was in a group of six girls called "the Victories" as class leaders.

Like me, Cam Lien is an Amerasian, born to an American serviceman during the Vietnam War. She looks more white than Asian, while I resemble my Vietnamese mother. When we met again after so many years, we began speaking about something we had both carried quietly for a long time. We talked about our experiences growing up and the discrimination we both experienced as mixed children. She was teased a lot as a child, but things got better as she grew older. I experienced similar challenges, though more through my brother, who looked much more Caucasian, with blond hair and fair skin. He was often bullied and beaten because of his appearance. Being a witness to his abuse was unbearably painful for me.

One day, our American foster parents received a call from the principal saying my brother had gotten into a fight. I was upset, so I asked him, "Why do you fight here? You already fought all your life in Vietnam. Was that not enough?" He replied, "In Vietnam, they called me 'mixed American,' and here they call me 'VC.'* I don't fit in anywhere." I was so enraged that I said, "Kill them, and I'll help you."

Like my brother, I felt caught between two worlds. I never felt at home in Vietnam. I wasn't respected or accepted there. My brother and I came to the United States because our grandmother believed we would have a better future here. But for many years, we felt stateless—outsiders in both places.

For the first thirty-one years of my life, I never felt like I had a true home—until I became a nun. Through spiritual practice, I gradually came to realize that I wasn't simply Vietnamese or American. I wasn't defined by any single identity. I'm not only a nun, a doctor, or any one thing. I am infinite and not confined by any single label.

To live peacefully in the world, we must first loosen the ideas we hold about who we are. The world exists within us, and we exist within the world. Being at peace with ourselves

* Viet Cong, communist.

is key to being at peace in the world. The practice of the Four Establishments of Mindfulness helps us arrive and feel at home, no matter where we are.

Returning to the Body

Learning to return to the body becomes increasingly important as we age. The breath offers us a simple and reliable way to come home to ourselves. In Zen practice, this returning is cultivated through the Four Establishments of Mindfulness, which encompass the body, feelings, mental formations, and perceptions. Let's explore each of these elements and how we can learn to be at home with them, starting with the body. The practice of mindful breathing (offered in Buddhist texts as sixteen exercises) is closely connected with the Four Establishments of Mindfulness. For instance, the breath is an integral part of the body, and the first two exercises are found in the Discourse on the Full Awareness of Breathing. The first exercise is: "Breathing in, I am aware that I am breathing in. Breathing out, I am aware that I am breathing out." The second exercise involves following the in-breath from start to finish, and doing the same with the out-breath.[5]

For trauma survivors, it isn't always easy to follow the breath. A monastic sister in our tradition shared that, after six years as a nun, she still struggled to follow her breath. Her father had been assassinated when she was a child, and trauma made it difficult for her to reconnect with her breath. She had to find reconnection through other parts of her body. Over time, as she healed along her path, she came to understand just how vital it is to be in touch with the breath.

In Chinese, the character for "breath" (息) has two parts: The upper part represents "from" or "itself," and the lower part represents "mind" or "heart." The breath originates from the mind and the heart. The breath is itself the mind and heart, true to the teaching of interbeing. When we are calm, the breath is calm. When we are anxious or upset, the breath becomes shallow or irregular. At the end of life, our breath often tells the final story. Nurses and doctors can often tell when death is near simply by listening to a person's breathing. This pattern, known as Cheyne-Stokes respiration, is marked by cycles of deep, rapid breaths followed by shallow breathing or periods of no breathing.

Trauma is often reflected in the way we breathe. Babies breathe deeply, their breath causing their abdomens to rise and fall, but as we grow older and experience stress or trauma, our breathing becomes shallower, often limited to the nostrils or throat. In mindful breathing, we observe whether the breath feels comfortable or uncomfortable.

To be present with what is with equanimity means not to be overwhelmed, to cling, to deny, or to avoid, whether our reality is pleasant, unpleasant, or neutral. A balanced mind can see things as they are, without prejudice or judgment. This equanimity is symbolized by Avalokiteshvara—the Bodhisattva of Deep Listening—standing serenely on a wave, untouched by the storm around her. It's not that there are no waves, but that we remain steady and calm amidst them.

Equanimity does not mean difficult emotions never arise. Sometimes they come as strong waves. The practice is not to suppress them, but to remain present as they move through us. I learned this lesson very personally early in my monastic life. I had just been ordained as a novice, and I was infamous for my tears. I was known then as the "crying nun" because I cried so much—not the "hugging nun," as I was called later on. I could cry anywhere, in public or private, which bothered some people. One day I mentioned to Thầy that I often felt the need to cry and asked whether it might be possible to build a soundproof room where people like me could cry freely without disturbing anyone.

Thầy responded with kindness and compassion, "Surely, my child, we can build a soundproof room for you to cry in. But do you think it may feed the pain and sorrow you carry?" Thầy left it at that. From that moment on, I began to practice crying mindfully. Instead of abandoning myself to the waves of emotion, I stayed with my breathing and felt my body as the tears flowed. Before that, I had often lost myself in emotions and memories like uncontrollable tidal waves. Crying with awareness, on the other hand, allowed me to remain present, mindful, and grounded. Afterward, I didn't feel drained. Over time, I cried less. Now when I cry, it is usually out of empathy for others. I no longer cry from despair or self-pity.

This experience helped me understand something very simple: When we stay with the breath and the body, even strong emotions can move through us without sweeping us away. When we focus on our breathing, our system naturally starts to harmonize. If we're overwhelmed by thoughts and feelings, they keep multiplying—like searching for something online, where one search leads to an endless list of related items. When we anchor ourselves in the breath, the mind stops generating endless thoughts, and the breath slows. The connection between breath and mind helps to calm both.

Our body holds valuable information about our state of being. When we disconnect from our body and get lost in thoughts and emotions, we often overlook these sensations. Many of us assume the brain is in charge, but in reality, 80 percent of sensory neurons send information from the organs to the brain, while only 20 percent go from the brain to the body.[6] This is why terms like "heart-brain" and "gut-brain" have emerged.

Instead of being caught in our intellectual mind, we can train ourselves to listen to our body. The heart, lungs, and gut provide us with feedback about our state. By placing our hand on our chest and following our breathing, we can check in with ourselves: "How am I breathing? How is my heart rate? How does my chest feel?"

Let's practice this together. Place your hand on your heart and notice how it feels. Is your heart rate fast or slow? Is your chest light or tight? Take a deep breath, saying to yourself, "I'm here for you. It's okay. I'm still here." Reconnecting with our body, we become more grounded and less overwhelmed by intrusive thoughts or emotions. This simple act of awareness helps us stay present and mindful, providing stability and peace throughout the day. Among all the gateways back to ourselves, the breath is perhaps the simplest and most reliable. It is always there, quietly waiting for us.

The Breath as Medicine

When we return to the body, we discover the breath is always waiting for us, and this rediscovery is simple, ordinary, and yet deeply healing. When befriended, the breath becomes a kind of medicine—one that the Buddha taught more than 2,600 years ago. The First Noble Truth is the presence of suffering. We begin by acknowledging it. The Second Noble Truth is that suffering has causes. The Buddha was known as the king of medicine—and rightly so. I studied medicine before I became a nun, and I can tell you that healing begins with acknowledgment of the pain that is present.

Upon seeing a patient, we start with a medical history. The first thing we ask is the patient's chief complaint: "I have had a cough for the last three weeks." "I have pain." "I haven't been sleeping." These are simple acknowledgments of suffering. Acknowledgment is essential, whether it's physical or mental suffering. Mindful breathing gives us a way to recognize what is present without turning away.

Next, we look into the causes. If a patient has had a cough for a month, we ask, "How did it start? Is it worse at night? Is there fever? Is anyone else in the household sick?" In the same way, the Buddha invites us to investigate the causes of our suffering. If we're always busy fighting, running, or denying our suffering, we never look deeply. We may even make things worse with unhealthy coping patterns.

Thầy said, in response to Shakespeare's famous line, "To be or not to be—that is *not* the question. The reality is to inter-be." Nothing exists in isolation. Everything is connected; everything exists in *interbeing*. It inter-is. For example, if you have a cough, you must consider family history and social history. An infection didn't arise in a vacuum. We don't generate viruses or bacteria from ourselves. We are always in relationship, influenced by and influencing others.

Though we often hold the illusion of a separate, fixed self, the truth is this: We inter-are. When you feel alone or isolated, remember: You are never truly separate. Take a breath. Notice the breath entering and leaving the body, exchanging air with the entire world. Know that everything changes. Your body is always changing. Your emotions and thoughts shift like clouds. The only things fixed are the ideas we cling to, thoughts we rehearse and reinforce until we can no longer see they are optional.

Contemplating interbeing helps us let go of rigid, dogmatic views. Even when we fight for noble causes, like protecting the earth, free speech, or justice, if we're caught in struggle—internally and with one another—we lose touch with the truth of interbeing and become less effective as a result.

Meditation is about making time to listen deeply. It is a bird with two wings: One wing is stopping; the other is deep looking. Only with both wings can the bird of insight soar. Stopping means halting the momentum of our mind. It means being fully present, as we are, right now—not as we wish to be, or how we wish the world to be. Mindful breathing helps us to do this; it brings us back. We simply recognize the in-breath and the out-breath. When we come back to the breath, we come back to the body. Our body—our gut, our lungs, our heart—tells us everything we need to know. In listening, we receive honest, immediate feedback about our state of being.

I cannot emphasize this enough: Mindful breathing is powerful medicine. The breath and the heart-mind are not separate. So, check in with your breath frequently. When you're walking, sitting in a noisy place, or waiting in line, put aside your phone. Don't escape from the present moment. Just return to your breath. Notice it. Befriend it. Allow it to support you in stopping so you can look deeply and benefit from the medicine you always carry: your breath.

Cultivating Trust

When we begin to return to the body and follow the breath, we start to see something clearly: Often we are the ones who take advantage of and take for granted our own body and mind, neglecting the conditions of happiness available to us. If we cannot love, appreciate, and take care of ourselves, how can we expect others to show us this respect? Likewise, without self-love and self-care, we will use, abuse, and take others for granted.

Often victims and perpetrators are seen as two separate entities. Yet the insight of interbeing shows us something more complex: The victim is in the perpetrator, and the perpetrator is in the victim. This does not excuse harmful actions, but it helps us understand their roots. Most perpetrators of physical, emotional, or sexual abuse have been wounded in childhood, and because they didn't know how to take care of their trauma, the patterns they rehearsed in their minds later became their speech and their actions. In a similar way, we may continue this cycle internally through the way we speak to ourselves: "You're stupid. You're worthless. I hate you!" Our inner speech can become another form of violence.

We should ask ourselves with honesty and humility: "Am I able to take care of myself? Am I able to be there for myself when I'm sad or angry? Am I able to hold myself in check?" We distrust others because we don't trust ourselves. If we have abandoned ourselves in pursuit of ambitions, drugs, or sex, how can we trust ourselves? Mistrust is healed by starting with ourselves. We learn to be there for ourselves through mindful breathing and mindful walking. With each step we take, we can say, "Come home, my dear." "I'm here for you." "Thank you for this body. Thank you for the eyes that can still see, for the body that is still functional, even though it may have gone through so much trauma." We learn to be there for ourselves, moment after moment, re-establishing what is referred to in psychology as a secure base. From this place of stability and care, trust can slowly grow again—first in ourselves, and then in others.

Perhaps we didn't have a healthy attachment to our parents, caregivers, or partners. We can begin to develop a healthy relationship with ourselves through consistent presence, building trust by no longer abandoning ourselves. When you can say, "Yes, I am being there for myself," trust becomes more natural. We can trust others because we can trust ourselves. Our spiritual practice leads us back to ourselves, helping us recognize our inner power—each one of us is already a Buddha, however part-time our awakened state may currently be. True to interbeing, to love oneself is to love others more kindly and deeply. Sometimes this shift happens slowly through practice, and sometimes it appears suddenly in a moment of insight.

Befriending the Perpetrator

The practices we've been exploring—interbeing, non-perception, non-expectation, and learning to be at home with ourselves—are not abstract ideas. Often their fruits appear slowly, ripening over many years of practice and lived experience.

They unfold in very ordinary, intimate moments, often in places we least expect. Sometimes they appear not as teachings or insights but in the middle of someone's lived struggle, when awareness begins to soften what once felt unbearable. What follows is one such letter, offered with honesty and courage, showing how befriending the parts of ourselves that we fear or reject can become a doorway to freedom.

> *Dear Sister Dang Nghiem,*
>
> *I listened to many talks of yours, and whenever you said we became our own perpetrator, I didn't get it. Since the beginning of the practice ten years ago, I can see that I have jealousy, and lately, it has been quite painful. But whenever jealousy was there, I tried to stay present.*
>
> *Yesterday, I was able to listen to my jealousy. And I learned she's really not bad, she shows up when it's me who is bad and mad at my inner Sangha. She just shows up to tell me, "Right now, you put all of us inner Sangha members down, you are disgusted by us. But we are not bad, we are not disgusting. You just learned to feel disgust toward us because you believed certain things happened because of us." And then I understand how mean I can be to myself, and I think, "Ah, this is what Sister Dang Nghiem means."*
>
> *And I celebrate this; it's so freeing! All those years of being jealous—I guess the feeling will keep coming up, but this understanding is quite exquisite to savor.*

Through this letter, we witness a quiet shift in perspective: What once appeared as an enemy within is revealed as a wounded part of the inner Sangha asking for understanding. Such understanding rarely comes all at once; it ripens slowly with patience and practice.

Child Logic

One of the deepest sources of self-blame begins very early in life. When we are children, we often try to make sense of difficult experiences with the limited understanding we have at that age. As we grow older, we may discover many of the painful beliefs we carry about ourselves were formed long ago, when we were children trying to make sense of painful events.

One time I sat with a group of teenagers, aged thirteen to fifteen, in a Dharma sharing circle that stuck with me. That day, many deep and vulnerable sharings arose. One girl voluntarily shared, "When my grandfather was dying, I was too young to know what to do. I was scared. I wish I had spent more time with him then." The next boy said, "I blame myself for my mother's death. She died of cancer. I was very sad, and after a while, I started to think it was all my fault." Another teen shared about feeling lost and awkward at school. Then the teen after him said, "I blame myself for my father's death. He died of suicide. I felt a lot of sadness and confusion and shame."

I let the teens share what was in their hearts without giving advice right away. A small bell was passed around the circle, and one sound of the bell was invited after each share. If the share was heavy, I asked for two sounds of the bell to be invited. It was important for them to share, and it was also important for them to practice returning to their breath to embrace the strong emotions in themselves and in their friends. Listening to the sound of the bell offered this opportunity, and a few mindful breaths enabled them to be truly present for the next person's sharing.

After everyone had a chance to share, I tried to address their pain and offer a way to practice with it. "You know, your parents had the best intentions in bringing you into the world," I said. "But as we have all discovered, our parents are imperfect. They make mistakes. So, we can practice taking better care of our parents inside of us. I want to tell you about my experience with my own parents. My parents brought me into the world, and then they just vanished. They weren't there to care for me. In my practice, I've learned to love my parents and to forgive them. Recently I had an insight while meditating on the five-year-old child in me and in my parents. We practice this guided meditation in every retreat, and I have done it many times over the years. However, this was the first time I heard my parents say, 'I'm so sorry. Please forgive me.' Hearing my parents ask for forgiveness after so many years meant so much! Even though the voice was in my own head, it brought me to tears."

To the two teenage boys in the circle, I said, "I want to tell you that your mother passed away because of her illness. She would never have wanted to leave you." To the other boy, I said, "And your father, he committed suicide because he saw no way out, but in no way was that your fault."

What I saw in this circle and have seen again and again is something I would call "child logic." In a child's logic, whenever something goes wrong in their body, in their experience, or in their parents' relationships, it is their fault. Children often blame themselves rather than others—bad things happen because they are bad. Children often tie themselves in knots in this way, with thoughts that torture them day and night. I could already see the damage done to the two boys in the circle. They looked pale and exhausted, shoulders hunched, eyes downcast, lacking the vitality of youth. Children who carry the burden of self-blame often grow into teenagers who feel depressed, withdrawn, and unsure of themselves. Without support, they may enter adulthood lacking confidence and afraid to engage fully in life and relationships.

Parents cannot be perfect, but we can be honest with ourselves and with our children. We can say, "I'm so sorry. I have limitations. It's not your fault your father and I are this way. You are innocent. We will try to change the situation."

I told the teens, "You can learn to take better care of your parents inside of you by taking better care of yourself. Exercise, rest, sleep, and eat better. Think positively so your body is healthier. Use mindful breathing and walking to embrace difficult emotions. You can help love and heal your parents inside of you. That is the kindest gesture and love that you can offer them."

As a spiritual practitioner, I have learned to love myself and, as a result, I have been able to care for and heal my parents inside me. Now when I think of them, I feel loving and grateful—I have no more thoughts of blame, shame, or confusion. My parents are liberated. When I dream of them, they are at peace. There is nothing I want more than to pass on these practices to young people, so they can heal themselves and the parents within them. In this way, the wounds of childhood do not have to define the rest of our lives. When we learn to release the self-blame of childhood, we give ourselves the freedom to live our lives more lightly and more fully.

LIVE BEAUTIFULLY, DIE BEAUTIFULLY—TODAY

Healing Child Logic

In this meditation, we gently turn toward the inner child logic that once helped us survive. This means turning toward the parts of us shaped by confusion, self-blame, or misunderstanding. This is a practice of presence, not analysis. We listen with the steadiness of an adult heart and the kindness of a trusted companion. You are in charge of the pace; if anything feels too much, you can always return to the breath.

Take a moment to arrive before breathing with the following phrases:

Breathing in, I befriend my in-breath.
Breathing out, I befriend my out-breath.
Befriending in-breath, out-breath

Breathing in, I befriend my body.
Breathing out, I smile kindly to my body.
Befriending my body, smiling

Breathing in, I befriend my inner child.
Breathing out, I smile kindly to my inner child.
Hello, my inner child. I'm smiling with you!

Breathing in, I listen deeply to the joyful thoughts and memories of my inner child.

Breathing out, I embrace my inner child's experiences.

Listening to my inner child, embracing

Breathing in, I become aware of whatever sadness, confusion, and challenges my inner child has experienced.

Breathing out, I relax and embrace my inner child's experiences.

Aware of challenges, embracing

Breathing in, I listen to my inner child's thoughts of self-blame and self-doubt.

Breathing out, I comfort my inner child: "You are okay. It's not your fault. I am here to protect you."

Listening to my child logic, comforting my inner child

Breathing in, I resolve to be more present and supportive of my inner child.

Breathing out, I send love to my inner child: "I love you. May you grow beautiful and strong. You deserve it."

Being present, loving my inner child

Breathing in, I am home with my inner child.

Breathing out, I heal my inner child.

At home with my inner child, healing together

Breathing in, I rest with ease in my in-breath.
Breathing out, I rest with ease in my out-breath.
Resting with ease in in-breath, out-breath

At Home in the Feelings

As we become more at home in our body and breath, we begin to notice another powerful dimension of our experience: our feelings. Learning how to relate to our feelings wisely is an important part of growing older with understanding and peace. This noticing is the second establishment of mindfulness. There are four kinds of feelings: The first is pleasant, which we naturally seek. The second is unpleasant, which most, if not all of us, try to avoid. The third type of feeling is neutral, and the fourth is mixed. A mixed feeling might be something like when you were a child and had a cut that formed a scab. Even though it was painful, you couldn't help but pick at it—there was something oddly satisfying about it, though it brought both pleasure and pain. In Vietnamese, we call this *thú đau thương*: "pleasure in pain." This mixed feeling can also be experienced with things like drug use that offer immediate pleasure but are later accompanied by physical and emotional suffering.

We move back and forth between these four feelings—chasing the pleasant, resisting the unpleasant, and avoiding what feels neutral or mixed. In this process, we grasp at or turn away from situations that stir them, becoming entangled in their rise and fall.

The Four Diligences are four ways of cultivating our inner lives that can help us tend to our feelings and become less triggered by or dependent on external circumstances. We invite wholesome seeds such as gratitude, love, compassion, and understanding to grow in our consciousness. At the same time, we avoid watering seeds of anger, fear, or despair by being mindful of the media we consume and the environments we place ourselves in.

Thầy often said a practitioner knows how to generate happiness at any time. We do this by being aware of the favorable conditions already available to us and cultivating gratitude for them. Simply saying, "Thank you for still being here. Thank you for giving me another chance" can make all the difference. You can say this to yourself, to a loved one, or to anyone who has helped you along the way. I practice gratitude often, especially toward my body. I am also deeply grateful to Thầy. If it weren't for him, I wouldn't be here today. I'd either be someone else or perhaps not even alive. Just this thought fills me with immense joy.

Now, let's turn to negative feelings—the uncomfortable and unpleasant ones that we often try to run away from. In truth, the more we try to avoid and push these feelings away, the more they are reinforced subconsciously.

To manage our feelings, we must first acknowledge them. Then we can learn to calm and embrace them. In fact, this applies to pleasant feelings as well as to negative or mixed ones. Mindful breathing can soothe and regulate our emotions so we are not tossed around like a yo-yo, constantly shifting with every change in circumstance. Instead, we can learn to experience our feelings with equanimity, recognizing them without being overwhelmed, clinging to them, or running away from them. Like waves on the ocean, feelings arise and pass, while our breath and awareness remain steady beneath them.

The Second Arrow

Zen teachings speak of two arrows. The "first arrow" is a misfortune or painful circumstance. As the saying goes, pain is inevitable, suffering is optional. Suffering becomes optional when we stop reacting to pain with the "second arrow"—the anger, denial, avoidance, or rehearsal that only intensifies the situation. I vividly remember feeling deeply offended when I heard Thầy say this for the first time. I thought, "What do you mean suffering is optional? I've suffered my whole life, and now you say it's optional?" Though I struggled to accept this, over time, I came to understand its truth.

Pain can be seen as an acronym: "Pay Attention Inside Now." Instead of seeking refuge in distractions like food, sex, work, the internet, or substances, we practice being with what is, with equanimity. We calm our feelings, whether they're pleasant, unpleasant, neutral, or mixed. To be at home with our feelings is to be grounded in our breath, our body, and our emotions.

It took me many years to understand this teaching. One moment in particular revealed its truth to me in a way I could never forget. One day, during my second year as a novice, I found myself alone in a field near the Lower Hamlet, crying uncontrollably. Overcome by intense emotions, I had been screaming and howling for a long time. Suddenly, a clear threshold appeared before me. I saw with stark and undeniable clarity that if I continued, even for just one more second, I could lose my sense of insight and cross into madness. I took the deepest breath of my life and sank to my hands and knees on the ground. Desperately, I prayed, "Please, help me never to suffer like this again. Never again!" It was the first time I made a resolute aspiration to never allow my suffering to spiral in that way again.

No one would claim they want to suffer. Yet with the practices of stopping and looking deeply we may see how we diligently water the seeds of suffering with negative and pessimistic thinking as well as the narratives we build around our experiences. When something happens, we tend to amplify it, turning it into a dramatic or traumatic story. Suffering can become an addiction—it's painful, yes, but it also feels familiar, almost comforting. Most of us actually have an addiction in common: our addiction to suffering.

Over the past twenty-five years as a monastic, I've made it my aspiration to transform my addiction to suffering. I still find myself slipping into the habit of nurturing unwholesome seeds within, but thankfully, I'm more aware of it now. I see this in how I view media. My attraction to Korean dramas in particular reveals a part of me that still carries some measure of addiction to suffering. Though crying mindfully in response to life's vicissitudes can be deeply healing, my inclination to watch dramas to trigger a good cry just waters my seeds of sadness, so I choose to resist the temptation to go down that path.

Some of us are drawn to action movies, others to horror or to comedies. Whatever the case, we can be mindful of what we feed our minds and actively stop watering seeds of suffering. Even when, out of habit, we continue watering those seeds, we can return to breathing, smiling, and nourishing ourselves. Though there are moments when I don't want to be present for myself, I show up for the community and follow our schedule, which helps me sit, breathe, and ground myself. With time, this diligence helps me move beyond negative states of mind and return to presence, both physically and mentally.

Recently, I received an email from a teenager I've been in contact with for several years. She experienced significant trauma as a child, but thankfully, she's now living in a loving home with adoptive parents. Still, she struggles with traumatic psychological episodes and self-harm. My story about the crying field resonated with her deeply and inspired her to make the same aspiration not to suffer again. Here's what she wrote:

> *Hi Sister D,*
>
> *In your book, you wrote that having a breakdown was the turning point in your life. You told yourself you'd never want to suffer like that again.*
>
> *All last week, I felt like I reached my turning point. It started with me getting really upset and banging my head multiple times against a wall. A few days later I had a flashback and I was screaming for at least an hour. I lost my voice—it was an insane experience. I was sweating and shaking the whole time. It was also very dangerous because my mom was driving.*
>
> *I told myself that I never ever want this to happen again. I started going to therapy twice a week to learn to manage these flashbacks.*

Her letter shows clearly that even the most painful moments can become turning points on the path of healing, when we learn to stop shooting the second arrow.

At Home in the Mind

Even when the body is still and the breath is calm, the mind continues its movement, forming thoughts, memories, emotions, and intentions. Learning to recognize these mental states as they arise is the third establishment of mindfulness—mindfulness of the mind and its mental states, also known as mental formations. Mental formations include feelings, perceptions, and other mental states that are constantly in flux, influencing one another. Mental formations like love, equanimity, jealousy, insecurity, hatred, or desire color how we experience the world. While mental formations may be distinctly classified for the sake of understanding, they are inherently and deeply interconnected.

As human beings, we have an instinct to focus on drama because it was once crucial for survival. Our ancestors needed to react quickly to threats like a tiger or a snake. Although most of us no longer face predators in the forest, our minds are constantly stimulated by modern life—notifications, news, and endless information—which repeatedly trigger the same stress responses, even more frequently than was the case for our ancestors. Through mindfulness, we can recognize each mental formation as it arises. When we are aware of a mental formation—whether positive or negative—we can breathe and stay present with it. We don't have to flee from it or be overwhelmed by it. Cultivating equanimity in this way gladdens the mind and can deepen as we age.

When we look more deeply into the mind, we see that it is composed of many mental formations. Some are stronger than others, shaped by our life experiences, habitual patterns, environment, and ancestral influences. Some ancestors may have stronger seeds of compassion and love, while others have passed down seeds of anger, jealousy, suspicion, or insecurity. These seeds are transmitted to us, and our practice is to recognize them without becoming overwhelmed by them.

Mental states such as guilt and shame are indeterminate—they can be either wholesome or unwholesome, depending on how we respond to them. For example, many of us, living in relative safety and privilege, may feel guilty or ashamed when we encounter suffering in the world. It's essential to acknowledge our privilege and use that awareness to cultivate compassion. If we take our blessings for granted, we risk becoming bitter, callous, or indifferent to others' suffering. If we channel our awareness into meaningful action through reflection, advocacy, and supporting those in need, we can transform guilt into a positive force for change. The same holds true for fear and uncertainty. By recognizing these mental states, breathing with them, and offering a steady smile, we can navigate difficult emotions without letting them control us, ultimately contributing to the well-being of ourselves, others, and the world around us.

Negative feelings and mental formations often give rise to more negativity, creating a vicious cycle of destruction. This explains the drastic transformations we see in people during times of natural disasters or war. Consider a young man from a good family, well-educated and thoughtful. Yet when he becomes a soldier and witnesses or engages in violence, he may become unrecognizable—a person who harms, destroys, and dehumanizes others. How does such a transformation occur? It happens because we carry all seeds within us; when we nurture the negative ones, they feed off each other.

When we recognize mental formations, a fundamental aspect of practice naturally appears: the capacity to let go. Letting go involves releasing not only arising thoughts and emotions but, on a deeper level, the tendency to cling to beliefs and views. It's similar to holding a fist too tightly—just as many of us grip our phones with unnecessary tension, we often carry tightness in our minds. True freedom lies in our natural ability to relax and release.

Letting go is essential at every stage of our practice: In the body, we calm the breath and release tension from our muscles. In our feelings, we recognize them, relax, and let them go. In the mind, we acknowledge and liberate mental formations. While we often believe consumption leads to happiness, true freedom and peace arise through letting go—finding spaciousness, ease, and presence within our bodies, thoughts, and emotions. We must regularly ask ourselves: "What kind of diligence am I practicing right now? What mental formations am I cultivating? How might I explore letting go?"

At Home in Perceptions

Even when our mind is calm, the way we interpret what we see can shape our entire experience. The fourth establishment of mindfulness is mindfulness of perceptions, which invites us to look closely at our views about ourselves, others, and the world.

Imagine standing in front of a tree. For one person, the tree may appear beautiful. It may evoke a fond memory of sitting beneath a similar tree with someone they loved. Just seeing it can bring feelings of joy and tranquility. For another person, the same tree might evoke fear. Perhaps a branch once fell and caused harm, or it reminds them of a painful event. Instead of peace, the tree brings tension or unease—same tree, different perceptions.

Our experiences, memories, and habits shape how we perceive the world, and this directly influences our quality of life.

It's not the object itself—the tree, the person, or the event—but how our mind interprets it. In mindfulness practice, we learn to recognize perceptions as they arise. When we care for this mind, which colors every aspect of our lives, we are less likely to get carried away. We see reality with greater clarity.

Our perceptions are constantly shaped by the environment around us. In modern life we are inundated with messages that encourage grasping and aversion. With just a click on a phone, we can make a purchase, and before we realize it, we've reacted to a craving. A friend once visited Deer Park Monastery with six pairs of shoes in her suitcase. I gently suggested that before impulsively buying another pair, she should pause, smile, and ask herself, "Do I really need this?" It's easy to get caught up in consumerism, but when we become aware of the perceptions and impulses that arise in the mind by observing the ebb and flow of experience, we can choose our responses more freely.

Not Fearing Other People

Our perceptions not only shape how we interpret situations, but also how we respond to the people around us. Once, a group of us monastics were walking in the city of Chicago right after a retreat. Out of nowhere, police appeared and pushed a man walking in front of me onto their car. It happened in a flash—sudden and frightening.

We continued walking. I noticed some men with gang insignia on the sidewalk ahead of us. Some of my monastic siblings kept to the very edge of the sidewalk to avoid them, but I simply walked down the middle.

The young men called out, "Hey!"

"Hello, brothers!" I replied.

One of them bowed, and I bowed in return. We smiled at each other.

Back at the temple, a brother asked, "Weren't you afraid?"

I replied, "No. They are people, just like us." Of course, during my five years of medical school, I had had the experience of working with incarcerated youth at the San Francisco Youth Guidance Center, some of whom had been gang members. I loved those young people as if they were my own brothers, which made it easy for me to extend that same compassion to gang members on the street.

When we don't feel safe within, we project that fear outward. Have you ever noticed that if someone avoids your eyes or pulls away from you, it hurts? Defensiveness is a reaction. Fear triggers defensiveness—in ourselves and in others.

It's essential to cultivate inner safety. When we feel secure inside, our perceptions are clearer. They are less reactive or judgmental, and this reduces harm—for ourselves and for others.

LIVE BEAUTIFULLY, DIE BEAUTIFULLY— TODAY

Entrusting

At a certain point, aging invites us to stop carrying everything alone. We can rest in what has supported us all along—life, ancestors, teachers, the earth. Entrusting is not giving up our strength; it is letting strength flow through us.

Take a posture that feels steady and natural, whether sitting, lying down, or standing. Let your hands rest where they are comfortable. Allow the breath to move the body on its own. Nothing needs to be held up, defended, or improved.

If you like, close your eyes or simply lower your gaze. Feel the support of the ground or earth beneath you. Let the body be held, just as it is. Let the breath be enough.

Following my in-breath and out-breath, I entrust
myself to the earth.

Following my in-breath and out-breath, I entrust
myself to my capacity to wake up.

Following my in-breath and out-breath, I entrust
myself to the wisdom of life.

Following my in-breath and out-breath, I entrust
myself to my mother inside me.

Following my in-breath and out-breath, I entrust
myself to my father inside me.

When we entrust ourselves, we do not disappear. We become part of something vast, steady, and alive. This is how we age with ease, how we live beautifully, and how we die beautifully each moment.

2

I am of the
nature to have
ill-health.
There is
no way to
escape having
ill-health.

Illness is not a punishment, nor is it a betrayal. It is the body's most honest language, calling our attention not only to its needs but also to the deeper, often neglected terrain of the spirit. Illness interrupts our plans, dismantles our illusions of control, and calls us back to what matters. We are taught to hide our pain and fight our limitations, but the Second Remembrance invites us to turn toward them instead. In illness, we are brought to the inexorable truth that being alive is being vulnerable. In the breaking down, we may begin to meet life more honestly, with humility, patience, and a fierce kind of grace.

The Body of Change: Every Cell Knows

Often, when we feel dissatisfied or disillusioned—with ourselves, our lives, our progress, or simply caught in darkness—we turn toward despair and then, inevitably, toward thoughts of death. Those "Ds"—dissatisfaction, disillusionment, darkness, despair, and death—seem to be intimately connected. So, the question becomes: In our daily life, how can we practice holding both the darkness and the light?

Even our cells carry the truth of impermanence: They live, serve, and naturally die so others may be born. We are programmed to grow old and to die, at a cellular level and at a cosmic level. As cells go through apoptosis, or programmed cell death, new cells are generated. By chance, sometimes a cell undergoes a mutation that prevents apoptosis; instead of dying, it continues to proliferate. That is cancer, which may bring about the demise of a person's physical body. The truth is that sickness can develop at any point, not just in old age. Many children also have terminal illnesses.

The Buddha taught clearly about suffering. Birth, death, old age, and sickness are not suffering in themselves. They are simply facts of life. Suffering arises when we deny or reject this truth. The body is meant to get sick, to grow old, and eventually to die. So, suffering does not come from the facts of life—birth, aging, illness, death—but from our relationship to them: our neglect, our denial, our rejection, our fear.

When we're healthy, we take it for granted. When we have energy, we waste it. Only when sickness and weakness arrive do we realize what we had—and wish desperately for our health back. In youth, when our energy is abundant, we often waste it pursuing things that are not meaningful. This is true not only for young people, but also for adults and even spiritual practitioners. How much time do we truly spend on what is meaningful—on taking care of ourselves, our families, and our communities? How much time is lost to distraction, to activities that don't nourish us? We must be willing to confront ourselves with honest answers to these questions.

The natural rhythm of old age and sickness makes our life possible. It makes future generations possible. The cycle of birth and death, of coming and going, enables life. Most of us suffer because we don't want to confront or accept this natural cycle. Spiritual practitioners are encouraged to contemplate old age and sickness regularly. Understanding illness and aging as part of a natural cycle transforms fear into non-fear. To live inside a fragile body is to walk daily with the awareness that everything can change in an instant. I know this in my bones.

Life Force

At Deer Park Monastery, there's a gigantic water tank to the north of our mountain. When I look at it, it reminds me of the life force within each of us. When we're young, our energy seems almost limitless. We spend it freely—on play, entertainment, work, relationships—believing it will never run out. We can stay up all night and still function the next morning. Over time, however, life has taught me our life force is like the water in that tank at Deer Park—finite. Some of us may be born with larger tanks, others with smaller ones, but all of us must learn how to cherish and conserve what we have.

When we misuse or neglect our life energy, we allow water to leak from the tank. Not knowing how to care for our bodies, our emotions, and our mental states creates holes in this inner reservoir through which our vitality can seep away. Anxiety, anger, sadness, doubt, and jealousy are all unskillful states that act like cracks through which life force drains, day and night. Over time, we find ourselves depleted.

I began to suffer from symptomatic hypotension (low blood pressure) in 2005 and then Lyme disease in 2011. Years of depression and unresolved grief had left me vulnerable, and when I was bitten by a tick, my body didn't have the strength to defend itself. I suffered from serious neurological symptoms as a result. Both the hypotension and the neurologic Lyme disease affected my short-term memory, recall, and concentration. I would read a page of a book and understand nothing at all. I couldn't even follow a simple scientific article. At times, I couldn't recall the name of a monastic sister whom I had lived with for years! It was frightening, to say the least. I took refuge in mindful breathing so fear and anxiety would not become second arrows, exponentially worsening the pain already present. The first arrow of illness and constraint causes pain, but a second arrow to the same wound causes suffering.

Our bodies are miraculous instruments of transformation. The same nervous system that once registered our fear or grief can also cultivate calm and compassion. Each breath is a living current of life moving through us, an invitation to begin again. When I contracted neurological Lyme disease, it became clear how my own unskillful ways had steadily drained my energy over the years. Thoughts like "I wish I were gone," or "Why am I still alive?" had drained my vitality and weakened my immune system.

This experience taught me the importance of awareness and self-care. Mindfulness of our true nature—that I am of the nature to grow old, to get sick, to die—encourages us to care tenderly for our energy. Our life force is shaped not only by the food we eat or the air we breathe, but also by the quality of our intention. A kind thought can steady our heartbeat; a harsh word can drain our vitality. Every moment of mindfulness replenishes our strength, just as every moment of distraction scatters it. Practicing with the Five Remembrances helps me stay in touch with both daily life and daily death, without needing to run away.

One cold morning on my way to the dining hall, I walked by an apple tree. It looked barren, lifeless, abandoned. I thought, "That is me." Then I remembered how, just three months earlier, Thầy had been there and the Sangha had gathered in great numbers. That same apple tree had been full of blossoms and imperfect, crunchy, sweet apples. Children stood under the branches trying to pick the fruit with sticks. Impermanence works in both directions—decay and renewal, I remembered. I took a deep breath and walked to the dining hall with a different state of mind, thanks to that apple tree.

The power of transformation and healing is already within us. Make time to sit still, walk quietly, and be a soulmate to your wounded inner child. Listen deeply to yourself. Take tender care of your thoughts, speech, and actions. Transformation takes place at the base, where views have been held tightly for many years without being questioned. When we care for our own well-being with understanding, we learn to care for others. Our calm breath can calm the person next to us; our steadiness can bring steadiness to the room. The life force in one body can awaken the life force in another.

Even when sick, the body is still trying to heal us. With mindfulness, we learn to appreciate the parts of the body that are healthy and those that are struggling. If we've had a near-death experience, we are still here—able to sit, speak, smile, and reflect. Recognizing the body's great healing potential helps us trust ourselves and touch non-fear. Resilience is already in us. We touch the sublime in a blooming flower, in the moonlight, and in our own quiet heart.

Caring for Loved Ones with Memory Loss or Dementia

Before we can care for another's confusion, we must learn to recognize our own. When we see clearly what happens in our own body—how fear tightens our breath, how stress steals our memory—we begin to understand how to walk beside someone who no longer remembers. Caring for another becomes much less about fixing and more about returning, again and again, to presence.

To care for others, we must first remember ourselves. A quarter of those over the age of eighty will experience dementia and some degree of cognitive decline. Dementia does not suddenly appear in old age. Its roots begin each time we live in forgetfulness, cut off from our breath, our body, and what is happening here and now. Forgetfulness is a subtle form of dementia; we lose contact with who we are, where we are, and what we're doing. We are swept away by fear, regret, distraction, and habit. Over time, the habits of forgetfulness may harden in us and become patterns, intersecting with neurological aging.

In the emergency room, doctors ask three basic questions: "What is your name? Where are you? What day is it?" These questions test alertness and orientation, but they can also be a spiritual practice. They call us back to the reality of our breath, our body, and time. When we are lost in our own thoughts, we too can pause and ask: "Where am I?" This question is a reminder to come home.

Modern science continues to confirm what the Buddha taught long ago: The body is intelligent. The heart, gut, and lungs send more messages to the brain than they receive. The body senses danger or safety before the mind understands. Anxiety appears first in the stomach, then in the mind, sadness first in the chest, fear first in the throat. Before we can speak of our suffering, our organs have felt it. When we learn to breathe deeply and relax the body, we are not escaping our experience—we are listening to it.

Depression, despair, grief, anger, and anxiety can disrupt sleep, impair memory, and even damage brain cells. The brain becomes overwhelmed, like a computer running too many programs at once. When stress becomes chronic, it quietly erodes our ability to think clearly, remember, or feel grounded. Healing is not possible in a body that stays tight and afraid. Like a wounded child, the nervous system cannot learn when it is punished or rushed; it can only learn when it feels relaxed and safe.

This is why mindful breathing is more than a mental practice—it is medicine. When the breath is calm, it sends signals of safety to the body. When the body relaxes, the mind begins to clear. The Chinese character for mindfulness (念) reflects this. It combines the character for "now" (今) with the character for "heart/mind" (心). Mindfulness means the heart-mind that is here, now. To breathe with awareness is to remember our life. To remember our life is to protect ourselves.

Caring for someone with dementia can stir up suffering. We may feel frustrated when we are forgotten, afraid of losing connection, or saddened by how the relationship has changed. These emotions are the second arrow that wounds us and the person we are trying to help. When we breathe for ourselves as well as for the one we care for, something softens. Our loved one is still here, even if the stories and names have faded.

With a beginner's mind, every moment can become meaningful. Even if it will be forgotten, the presence we offer is real while it is given. Presence is never wasted. When we spend time with loved ones who are experiencing memory loss, we can silently say:

Breathing in, I know you are still here with me.

Breathing out, I smile with you.

Thank you for all the moments we have shared.

We do not need someone to remember us in order to love them. In the light of mindfulness, connection is not made of memory. It is made of true presence.

Rewiring the Brain

Scientists speak of the brain's "neuroplasticity"—its capacity to change and form new connections throughout life. In the same way, the more often we repeat a thought, reaction, or habit, the stronger its pathway grows in the brain. This is why selective watering of the seeds in our consciousness is vital. If we continually water seeds of irritation, hatred, fear, or despair, those pathways widen and become our default. If instead we nurture joy, compassion, and gratitude, those become the routes our mind naturally takes. What we choose to water will sprout and grow; what we neglect will wither. Daily mindfulness practice is the tending of these inner seeds. Neuroplasticity is often described as a marvel of modern science, but the Buddha taught this insight long ago.

The hopeful truth is that change is always possible. Even if we have spent years reinforcing a negative pattern, the brain can still be rewired. A neglected path in the forest can be cleared and walked again; so too can neglected seeds of kindness or patience be brought to life.

Breathing in, I touch the seed of calm in me.
Breathing out, I water it with care.

This is the science and the art of mindful living: Every breath, every thought, every action lays down another track in the brain. Over time, these tracks become who we are. By choosing carefully what we reinforce, we shape the person we are becoming, and the ancestor we will one day be. Illness reminds us our bodies and minds are deeply intertwined. Healing does not end with the body—it continues in the tender terrain of the heart.

Die Quickly!

Thầy taught us to practice recognizing and releasing the deeply held misperceptions that cause us to suffer, day by day, moment to moment. Early in our monastic life, a younger sister from my ordination family said to Thầy in front of everyone, "I feel like I am dying, dear Thầy." Thầy responded, "Good, die quickly!" I gasped, my mouth open in shock. With a gentle tone, Thầy added, "So the baby Buddha may be born."

On this monastic path, I have learned to allow my false perceptions to die more quickly so I may live more freely and beautifully. For so long, I thought I was my views, thoughts, and feelings. I clung to them without realizing they engendered and perpetuated constant turmoil and internal strife. Even as I discovered this paradox, I remained absurdly attached to them, even addicted. Breath by breath and step by step over many years, I trained my mind to relax and release these waves of thoughts and emotions. Slowly, the present moment proved to be more pleasant and real than those waves.

Thầy was gentle and patient, but he also unhesitatingly used the sword of wisdom to cut right through wrong views. For instance, when I contracted Lyme disease, I was deeply upset by some people's suspicion and negative reactions. In a moment of frustration, I poured all the pain and injustices I had been holding inside out to Thầy. He listened quietly for a while, then gently said, "My child, you are being a victim. Don't play the role of a victim." His words deflated my anger and frustration, showing me a better way to care for myself.

In Health and Sickness

People of all ages can fall ill. Illness often catches us by surprise, and many of us are unprepared for it. For that reason, it is just as important to care for our health when we are well as when we are unwell. When we are healthy, our energy is strong and abundant, and we often become absorbed in work and activity, overlooking the different kinds of energy arising in us throughout the day. With mindfulness, we learn to find balance. While we may know intellectually that we are of the nature to be ill, deep reflection before and during illness can cultivate non-fear. In Buddhism, non-fear is the greatest fruit of practice. To face illness and death without fear allows us to live meaningfully, purposefully, and wholeheartedly until our last breath.

Practicing mindfulness while we are still healthy and clear-minded helps strengthen our mental stability so it will be there for us as a vital support in times of illness and vulnerability.

Serious illness can disturb our trust in our own body. A cancer diagnosis, for example, can provoke powerful stress responses. One response is "fight"—feeling compelled to battle the illness with every possible resource, no matter the prognosis. Another response is "flight"—denying the diagnosis or avoiding the topic entirely: "There's nothing wrong with me," or "I don't want to think or to talk about it." The third response is "freeze"—shutting down and disconnecting from our body and our life. When this happens, we may feel as though the body is an enemy trying to destroy us. These responses may initially protect us, but eventually they drain our energy and deepen suffering.

Sometimes we may wonder, "How can I love my body when it has caused me so much pain? How can I trust a body that has been the source of trauma?" These questions are unkind to the body; they stir stress hormones and increase suffering. In such times, reconnecting to the body is crucial. We can choose to pause, breathe, and speak intimately with the body, "Hello, my dear body. I know you are doing your best. Thank you for supporting me. Help me take better care of you."

Speaking with tenderness and love to our body is true kindness. It invites healing rather than tension and resistance. Following our natural in-breath and out-breath helps the mind return to the body, rest in it, and touch the powerful life force still present within. We can also gently scan the body from head to toe; wherever there is tension or pain, we breathe into it, soften, and offer gratitude. Healing requires safety and relaxation. It requires love. Relaxing the body and breathing with tenderness allows healing to take place. Gratitude is medicine for the body and mind. Even when we are sick, there is always something functioning well. By appreciating what we have, we gladden the mind and strengthen the body. Disease arises from many conditions—genetic, environmental, social and lifestyle-related. Understanding this helps us cultivate compassion and patience for ourselves. It's important to maintain a grateful and relaxed mindset, as this gives our body more energy and space to heal.

The truth is, life and death are not separate. An apple, no matter how perfect it may appear from a distance, will show blemishes if you look closely enough. We suffer because we deny and fear this truth. If we can greet the age spots, wrinkles, and changes in our body with tenderness and understanding, even when they herald illness, acceptance gradually blossoms in our heart. We recognize that it is not how long we live, but how deeply we live and love each day that matters.

In critical medical conditions, our priorities may become clearer. Breath becomes precious. The ability to speak, sit up, walk, and use the restroom by ourselves becomes a miracle. Illness reminds us what truly matters. Those who love us will carry us forward. The Five Remembrances remind us that even as this body disintegrates, our actions, our words, and the love we have shared continue. When we understand this, spiritually and viscerally, every day becomes infinite—whether we have one day, one year, or twenty years left to live.

A former cancer patient once shared with me, "My doctor told me I'm in remission. He said I can go live my life now—but I don't know how." I told him, "Perhaps this is the first time you have been invited to truly see your life. How have you been living? How do you want to live now?" No doctor can answer that question for us.

Only by facing illness honestly can we learn to live more deeply. When we live deeply and die deeply each day, we embody the wisdom of non-fear. True healing is to cherish each moment, to reconcile and release regrets, and to embrace all that's coming and going with non-fear.

Rain: The Coolness of Nirvana

Illness is not only change of the body; it is an opportunity for the heart and mind to mature. I once witnessed this ripening of practice in a young man named Rain. I visited Rain in his home in 2017. He had been living with cancer for nearly six years. Two months before he had been hospitalized, his wife left him. When I asked how he felt about her, he said quietly, "I don't have any bitterness. I wish her happiness. I'm actually glad things turned out this way, because now I have time with my mom and dad in my last days."

Rain spoke with joy about a trip to Vietnam he had taken soon after his diagnosis. "There are so many things I want to do!" he said with the bright eagerness of someone who still loved life deeply. Gently, I asked, "A time may come when your body will not be able to continue. Are you okay with that?" He smiled, calm and luminous, as he answered, "I will enjoy every moment I have."

When I visited Rain again in the hospital, he was nearing the end of his life. He wanted to hear the Five Mindfulness Trainings. He was too weak to sit up on his own, so we helped prop him up, and he joined his palms reverently as I read the Five Mindfulness Trainings. His breathing was labored, but his attention was unwavering. Every word seemed to enter him like cool water.

In his final moments, Rain could no longer speak. He gazed at his mother, father, brother, and sister with a tenderness that spoke more clearly than words. His mother, in a steady voice that only love could sustain, whispered, "I give you permission to let go. It's going to be okay. Your dad and I will care for your brother and sister, and they'll care for us. You don't need to worry." Then she added softly, "Wait—could you give me one last smile?" And he did. With that radiant smile, he took three gentle breaths and passed away—peacefully, tenderly.

Later, his mother told me, "It saddens me that he's no longer with me physically, but I do not suffer, knowing he died peacefully." Rain had entered the coolness of Nirvana—the deep peace that comes when grasping and fear fall away—long before his final breath. His mind had grown quiet; his heart, unbound.

Once, traveling with Thầy and our community through Jakarta, we passed a funeral home named "Nirvana." We all smiled. The name, though perhaps chosen for commercial reasons, carried a deep truth: Nirvana is not about escaping death. It is about finding peace within it. When our discriminations, preferences, attachments, and aversions settle, the mind becomes vast and cool. We see life as it truly is: beautiful, fleeting, and whole.

Rain embodied this. His peace was not the denial of pain but the acceptance of it. He had nothing left to long for, and therefore nothing left to lose. His joy was steady, like a clear flame that no wind could shake. Even as his body weakened, his spirit was alive with gratitude.

One Toe Wiggles

"One Toe Wiggles" was the last piece of calligraphy Thầy wrote before he suffered a stroke in October 2014. Around that time, he began to feel weak and found it difficult to walk. One day, his big toe became swollen. Thầy was taken to the hospital, but the doctors didn't believe they could do anything. They did not suspect a stroke was imminent—it might have been a thromboembolism, a clot in a vein, that caused the swelling.

That evening, at 8:00 p.m., Thầy told his attendants that his toe could wiggle, and everyone rejoiced. The next day, Thầy asked to be brought back to his hermitage. Once back in the quiet of his hermitage, Thầy composed a simple and profound piece of calligraphy: *"One Toe Wiggles."* Beneath it, he wrote in French the name of the hospital and the date—October 12, 2014, at 8:00 p.m.

This was the last calligraphy ever written by the Zen Master. It beautifully reflects the essence of Thầy's teaching: The conditions for happiness are always available. If even one toe can still wiggle, that is a moment of joy. If two toes can wiggle, the happiness is doubled. No matter our circumstances, if we can remember that one toe still wiggles, or even one finger, we can smile. In that awareness, gratitude and happiness arise naturally.

LIVE BEAUTIFULLY, DIE BEAUTIFULLY— TODAY

Hello, Sadness. Hello, Fear.

Sometimes, people ask me, "Sister D, why do you smile so often?" I reply, "Sometimes I smile because I'm happy, but most of the time I'm smiling at my own negative and crooked thoughts." Known for being a serious person, I've learned to approach my thoughts and feelings with humor so I don't take them—or myself—too seriously.

Whenever I can breathe and smile to the turbulence within, I touch calm and non-fear. Many of us experience fear or depression when facing severe illness or a near-death experience. In those moments, we can practice smiling gently with the feelings and thoughts that arise: "Hello, sadness. Hello, fear. I'm here for you."

Breathing in, I greet my thoughts and feelings.
Breathing out, I smile and soften them, like caring for a child.

Instead of drowning in thoughts, we return to the body:

Breathing in, I'm aware of my forehead.
Breathing out, I relax my forehead and smile.

We scan the face and smile with gratitude for what still works well. We continue through the body—shoulders, arms, legs—quietly saying, "Thank you. I appreciate you. I know you are doing your best."

If there's discomfort, we can practice:

Breathing in, I'm aware of this pain.
Breathing out, I offer gratitude to my body for supporting me.

Sometimes this awareness follows us into places we did not choose—places where fear may tighten the body and breath, like hospital rooms. Hospitalization can be frightening, yet with mindfulness we can remember it as a place of support rather than trauma, giving rise to gratitude for the staff, family, and conditions that help us recover.

Whether walking, standing, sitting, or lying down, the body is always in contact with something that holds it. When you walk, feel the contact with the earth and offer a gentle smile: "Thank you, Mother Earth, for carrying me." When we sit, walk, or lie down with awareness, Mother Earth becomes our home. We feel safe.

We can quietly say, "I have arrived. I am home." This practice helps us live more deeply, supporting our immune system and body. If we can breathe and smile, we are already healing.

Illness of the Heart

In the years I have accompanied practitioners, I have seen that illness does not arise only in the body. Sometimes we suffer from emotional and relational illness—wounds that come from fear, dependency, and the longing to be loved. A young woman once wrote to me in great distress, feeling lost in a relationship where she felt unseen and negatively compared to others. Her letter was full of confusion, longing, and self-blame. She believed if she just loved harder, sacrificed more, or waited longer, she might finally be chosen.

As I read her words, I could feel how her suffering came not from the other person alone, but from the deep-rooted perception that she was unworthy unless someone else confirmed her value. I wrote back to her with the same tenderness I offer my own younger self, telling her our worth is not borrowed from anyone—that love built on insecurity cannot bring peace, and that no path requiring the loss of dignity can lead to freedom. I encouraged her to return to her breath, to her own solidity, and to the child within her who longed to be held—not by another person, but by her own acceptance and understanding.

Over time, she saw more clearly. She realized what she was calling "love" was often a plea: "Please see me. Please save me. Please make me whole." When she touched this insight, her suffering softened. She no longer begged for someone to choose her. Instead, she began choosing herself—day by day, breath by breath. The moment she did, the relationship resolved naturally. Her clarity, not the other person's decision, freed her.

Stories like this remind us that the deepest illnesses are sometimes our wrong perceptions: the belief that we are not enough, the fear of being alone, illusions that our happiness depends on another person. Mindfulness helps us see these knots with compassion. When we hold our pain with understanding, a new kind of health rooted in self-respect, stability, and love that does not harm becomes possible.

The Body Speaks the Dharma

Suffering shows itself in many forms—sometimes through our relationships and perceptions, and sometimes through the body itself. Illness, too, becomes a profound teacher when we know how to listen. During a three-month retreat in 2021, I was sick for a month and a half. I experienced severe back pain accompanied by spasms—it felt as though my back was a flap of muscles, spastic and trembling violently. When the spasms subsided, a deep, visceral pain remained. I wondered to myself, "Could I have cancer?"

I breathed with the pain. I endured the pain. Yet I did not suffer psychologically. I asked myself, "What would I do if this were cancer?" And in that moment, I felt I had lived my life the best I could. I wouldn't have changed anything.

Illness can be an opportunity, an invitation to embrace our condition and to touch the reality of aging and the fragility of our health. It can motivate us to reconcile and bring resolution to unfinished matters within ourselves, with those around us, and with our family and friends. The inevitability of illness reminds us not to wait for later.

Before I go on a long trip—and even before I leave my room—I make sure it's clean and tidy. I do this with the awareness that I may not return; I don't want to leave a mess for someone else to take care of. This simple habit is a daily contemplation of impermanence. It liberates me from the energy of fear and allows me to truly live.

An intense fear of death can be a sign we're not yet living deeply, that we haven't truly touched life. We fear the unknown, but when we live with presence and awareness, we begin to see that death is not far away—every in-breath and every out-breath is born and dies. Looking deeply in this way, we can free ourselves to be truly present. If we live with peace and no regrets, we can say, "Tonight, when I go to sleep, I may not wake up—and that's okay, because I know I've done my best." To me, that is living beautifully, and dying beautifully, in the midst of daily life.

LIVE BEAUTIFULLY, DIE BEAUTIFULLY— TODAY

Befriending the Body of Change

Sit comfortably. Let your shoulders soften and your hands rest gently in your lap. Breathe naturally. When you feel ready, I invite you to explore the following phrases in rhythm with your breath:

Breathing in, I befriend my in-breath.

Breathing out, I befriend my out-breath.

Befriending in-breath, befriending out-breath

Quietly ask yourself, with kindness:

What is my name?

Where am I?

What day is it today?

Let the answers settle like soft light in your body.
Now, bring the light of awareness to your body:

Breathing in, I am aware of my head and face.
Breathing out, I release all tension.

Breathing in, I am aware of my shoulders and chest.
Breathing out, I soften and smile.

Breathing in, I feel my whole body.
Breathing out, I relax completely.

In each moment, cells in this body are born and die. Change is not an enemy; it is life itself.

Breathing in, I touch the truth of impermanence.

Breathing out, I smile to this truth.

Place a hand on your heart and say silently: "Hello, my dear body. Thank you for doing your best. Let us take good care of each other."

Breathing in, I touch the seed of calm in me.

Breathing out, I water it with care.

In, calm. Out, careful watering.

This body is fragile, and it is precious.

Breathing in, I cherish this moment.

Breathing out, I live beautifully, today.

From Coping to Captivity: How Addiction Begins

Many addictions begin as attempts to cope with overwhelming experience. When faced with a crisis, human beings instinctively respond to survive. These responses usually fall into the now familiar categories of fight, flight, freeze, or fawn. What begins as the body's wisdom—its attempt to endure—can, without awareness, continue in the body long after the danger has passed, leaving us frozen, exhausted, or reactive.

Our coping strategies are also shaped by our environment. The patterns we witness in our families and how others cope with pain often become our own. If we grow up seeing those around us turn to alcohol, drugs, or pornography to escape their problems, we may adopt similar behaviors. Today, many children and teenagers turn to the internet as a means of self-regulation, numbing themselves from the emotional turmoil in their homes—what many intuitively call "escape." Addiction becomes a way to manage what feels unbearable, both within and around us.

Whatever helped us survive a difficult experience can, over time, solidify into a habit—rehearsed so many times it becomes second nature. Addictions—to substances, work, sex, or screens—often begin as a way to avoid confronting pressure or pain that feels overwhelming. Over time, these coping mechanisms can become fixed patterns that no longer support healing, even when our circumstances have changed.

As adults, the wounded child within us may still react, seek safety, and cling to old patterns of responding to stress, even if the very mechanisms that once protected us now bring persistent suffering to our lives. Viewing addiction in this light helps lift the shame, guilt, helplessness, and blame often placed on those struggling with it. Looking deeply, we see we have all relied on coping mechanisms of one kind or another—some helpful, some less harmful, some simply less visible. In recognizing this, we cultivate understanding and compassion for ourselves and one another.

We also gain hope and confidence in our ability to heal addiction. Instead of focusing only on symptoms, we begin to sense the deeper patterns beneath them. Addiction is only the visible surface of an invisible wound. Much of this process lives below conscious awareness, in the deeper layers of the mind and body.

I suffered from depression for years—unable to articulate it, simply feeling it in every part of my body and mind. At times I'd feel melancholic or lethargic, drawn to sad songs, novels, or dramas. Outwardly, my life seemed normal, but something lurked beneath the surface. With years of mindfulness practice, I rarely experience that excruciating pain anymore. I've learned to trust my store consciousness—the deeper layers of the mind—to do its work. The best I can do is continue my practice and follow my community's daily schedule to keep my mind steady and grounded. I still feel melancholy at times, but it no longer overwhelms me or crushes me as the depression once did.

I've never felt so safe and loved from deep within as I do now. I have a path. I am changed. Each time we meet our pain with awareness instead of avoidance, the body learns that it is no longer alone. When we begin to recognize addiction as the body's attempt to find safety, compassion naturally arises. These truths of how we live and the impact this has long after we're gone are not abstract. Healing begins in small moments of recognition, where survival patterns are slowly transformed through care and attention.

When Craving Becomes Illness

Addiction is not a moral failure. It is an illness of the body and mind, a habit energy that once protected us. When the nervous system does not feel safe, it reaches for whatever brings temporary comfort—substances, work, entertainment, relationships, or even obsessive thinking. These patterns do not arise in isolation; they grow from our personal history, our family, and the culture we live in.

Just as illness arises from many conditions, so does healing. Mindfulness helps the body return to safety, and community helps the heart remember it is not alone. When we breathe with craving instead of obeying it, the body learns another way to soothe itself. The nervous system begins to trust the present moment. This is the beginning of freedom.

And just as no one becomes sick alone, no one heals alone. A safe environment is medicine. Sometimes this means changing where we live or who we spend time with, but often it begins more simply: a friend who listens, a community that practices, a corner of a room where we breathe each day, a quiet space within ourselves where we can return.

Addiction alters the brain's pathways. The Buddha understood the biology of craving long before neuroscience gave it a name. The mind seeks what brings relief, whether it is wholesome or unwholesome, beneficial or unbeneficial. Neural circuits strengthen through repetition, like trails deepened by many footsteps. Craving survives not because we are weak, but because the body learns to grasp in order to survive.

The Buddha once asked:

"What is the one thing that, if uncultivated, brings suffering?"

The mind.

"And what is the one thing that, if cultivated, brings happiness?"

The mind.

This is not a moral teaching; it is biological wisdom. Mindfulness interrupts the momentum of craving long enough for the brain to form another pattern. Every breath that meets craving without feeding it forms a new neural pathway. To support this transformation, we need not struggle or suppress. We simply learn where to place our attention. There is mindfulness that heals, and mindfulness that harms. Attention itself can feed addiction or dissolve it. When the mind consumes disturbing images, intoxicating media, or environments that inflame craving, the nervous system learns agitation. When our attention is grounded in breath, beauty, compassion, and community, the nervous system learns peace instead of chaos and fear.

Zen teachings speak of "right" mindfulness. "Right" here is not a moral judgment, but means something more like "wise," "skillful," or "beneficial." Right Mindfulness is not simply "being aware." It is choosing what we nourish with awareness. "Wrong" mindfulness grasps and intensifies craving; Right Mindfulness steadies the body and clears the mind. We can train our actions, our speech, and our thoughts to calm us instead of scatter us. We can teach the body not to fear its own feelings. Healing begins when we stop waging war against our craving and start caring for it.

Breathing in, I feel the craving without giving in to it.

Breathing out, I offer it safety through a stable posture and tender energy.

Craving begins to soften. The body remembers another way.

Illness, addiction, and trauma cannot always be cured, but they can be cared for. We do not need to reject or scold the craving body. We hold it like a child who once learned to grasp in order to survive. When the body trusts our kindness, healing slowly takes root.

The Body Knows

Tolerance and sensitization to the objects of our addiction can cause immense suffering. At the level of the body, what begins as relief can gradually become dependence. Over time, the same substance or behavior no longer brings the same relief. Our body has built *tolerance*. To feel even mildly elevated, we now need more. Over time, without it, we don't even feel steady at all—we may feel increasingly agitated, depleted, or low. That deep, sickening sense of restlessness, angst, pain, and emptiness becomes unbearable. So, we no longer use the substance to feel good, we use it just to stop feeling terrible. It's not pleasure that drives us anymore, but a desperate need to escape the crushing discomfort in our body and mind.

Many assume people use drugs to feel good, but the truth is, they often just want to feel normal—to escape psychological pain and, later, the added torment of physical withdrawal. As the brain builds tolerance, it becomes less responsive to the same stimulus, requiring stronger doses to achieve the same effect. At the same time, the brain becomes *sensitized*, meaning that even a small dose—or merely a reminder of it, such as an image, sound, scent, or place—can provoke an intense craving. In those moments, obtaining the object of addiction can feel like the only way to quiet the storm within.

Alongside these physiological changes, many of us also grapple with denial. We may refuse to acknowledge a deeper distress and turn to drugs to mask it. We may be living with physical pain we feel unequipped to face and rely on substances—including prescription medications—to numb the discomfort, only to find ourselves caught in addiction. We justify our actions, which makes it harder to seek help or recognize a way out. A social worker once told me that "denial" can be understood as an acronym: Don't Even kNow I Am Lying. The truth is, many of us wholeheartedly believe the lies we tell ourselves.

Addiction is not limited to substances. The same patterns can be seen in our relationship to stimulation itself. We reach for our phones in the morning before we breathe deeply, before we greet a loved one. In public transportation, at a restaurant, at home—everyone is focused on a screen. Children are babysat by tablets, and teenagers use games and movies for escape and self-regulation. The body sits still, but the mind is constantly in motion. We no longer remember who we are, where we are, or what time it is. We are training ourselves to forget.

This collective forgetfulness has consequences. When the mind is continually preoccupied, many parts of the brain are neglected. The circuits of empathy, attention, and patience that once connected us to each other begin to atrophy. We see rising rates of depression, anxiety, rage, addiction, even suicide.[7] In a sense, we are losing the capacity to rest in the present moment. The constant stress and fragmentation of attention erode both memory and mood. Back in the '80s and '90s there was a TV commercial that said, "This is your brain" while showing an egg. Then the egg hit a hot pan with a sizzle: "This is your brain on drugs." Today it could read: "This is your brain on electronics." Fried.

We can begin to notice how the nervous system is shaped by what we repeatedly do. The brain adapts to what we use most. Hours on screens train certain circuits and leave others underfed. I once met a young mother with a beautiful child in a stroller. "She's been playing with this cup of leaves for the last hour and a half," the mother told me. That's wonderful! Ninety minutes of happiness with a cup and some leaves. When a child plays with leaves, the whole sensory system awakens to engage with sound, texture, smell, color, and the living world. With a screen, it's mostly staring, passively receiving. Over time, the brain tunes up what is used and prunes away what is not.

As certain capacities strengthen, others weaken. We may become less able to feel, to rest, to stay present with discomfort. The nervous system becomes more easily overwhelmed, and recovery takes longer. This contributes to rising levels of anxiety and depression. We may notice that being behind a screen feels easier than being face-to-face, and that presence requires effort. This is not a personal failure, but a reflection of how the body has been conditioned. The body always tells the truth. Let it guide your next choice toward something more alive, more real, more human. Shallow breath, a tight chest, or a restless mind are meaningful messages, not inconveniences or failures. When we notice these experiences, we can turn gently toward the body: turn off the phone, step away from the screen, lie down if needed, place a hand on the belly, and breathe. Even a few breaths of conscious presence can begin to settle the storm.

We can take time away from our devices and let the brain rest and rewire. Reach out for human interaction. Invest in relationships. Try new expressions—art, movement, language, culture. In time, the nervous system relearns safety, rhythm, and connection. Choose touch, movement, eye contact, silence, breath, and your body will remember. We don't have to be perfect. We only have to be willing to listen to the craving, to the ache, to the tremor, and to meet it with care. The body knows. If we honor its signals and choose one small human act at a time, we find our way home.

When we listen to the body, healing begins at the level where suffering is first felt. It is not abstract. It is lived, sensed, and gradually transformed through attention and care.

Touching Trauma with Compassion

Not long ago, I offered a consultation to a lay friend who was staying at the monastery for two weeks. As we sat together in silence, I could sense from her body language that she needed to share something far beyond the questions she had prepared.

After a moment of hesitation, Tammy finally said, "When I was five years old, I was pinned down by five boys. How do I live with that?"

As she recounted what had happened, her hands started to tremble. I gently placed my hands over hers, which were resting on her knees. Soon her whole body began to shake violently. This wasn't a memory she was merely recalling—she was reliving it.

I said softly, "You don't need to talk, my dear. Just breathe." Then I embraced her.

Her trembling intensified—first in her hands, then her knees, then throughout her entire body. I said, "Let's sit on the floor," and carefully helped her down from the chair. Holding her close, I cradled her in my arms as she curled into the crouching posture of a small child. I rocked her gently, back and forth. In my arms, she was once again that five-year-old girl, shaking and trembling with fear and pain.

Animals, when they are chased or narrowly escape death, often tremble vigorously afterward. I once saw a bird fly into a glass window and fall to the ground. After a moment, it stood up, and its entire body shook for quite some time before it flew away. Humans experience something similar after a car accident, a fall, or even a sudden shock. The body's natural tremor response releases physical and emotional tension. We rarely allow our bodies to complete this response, though. More often, we get up as quickly as possible and move on as though nothing happened.

Something deep within me knew Tammy needed presence—a firm, loving embrace, steady and grounded—not words. So, I held her tightly, simply being there with her as her body shook and shook.

Gradually, her trembling began to still. Remaining curled in that childlike position, Tammy whispered, "Thank you. Thank you. Thank you."

I continued holding her, gently rocking her back and forth, and replied, "Thank you. Thank you for surviving all these years. Thank you for all the efforts you've made."

I sensed it was her inner child who thanked me, and I spoke directly to that precious child when I said, "Thank you for trying so hard, for surviving, for doing extraordinary things despite all the pain, shame, guilt, and sadness you've carried for so long."

The little girl responded softly, "I was just following the boys. . . . I didn't know any better. I was just a little kid."

After her body became calm, I gently shared with her that those young boys must have seen what they did somewhere. They were imitating something, reenacting violence they had once witnessed or experienced. In that sense, they too were victims.

The next day Tammy told me, "I feel like my inner child just burst out of me yesterday. She wanted to be seen, wanted to be held, but I didn't know how to do that for myself." She expressed gratitude for my showing her how to embrace her own wounded child so she can care for herself. She felt deeply connected to herself and her inner child now, and so much lighter.

This is transformation at the base—true healing.

Stroke of Insight

The Second Remembrance teaches us that we are of the nature to become ill. Illness can arrive suddenly, interrupting our plans and revealing how fragile the body and mind truly are. Sometimes, in the midst of that disruption, unexpected insight can arise.

Neuroanatomist Jill Bolte Taylor spent her career studying the brain. In her thirties, she experienced something she had studied for a long time: a massive hemorrhagic stroke in her left hemisphere. As her language, memory, and ability to move slipped away, she became acutely aware of her brain shutting down.

What astonished her most was not the loss, but what opened up in its place. With her left brain offline, her right brain came to the foreground. In those hours, she described experiencing herself as pure energy, without boundary or a separate self. Time dissolved. The chatter of thought fell silent. She later said she touched nothing less than Nirvana—a profound peace and oneness where all emotional baggage dropped away.

Of course, she also knew she needed help. Her scientific training told her that her life was at risk. And yet, alongside the urgency and fear, she was carried by a sense of vastness and liberation that she would never forget.

Her account offers a modern parable for the teachings of mindfulness. In our world, the left brain—analytical, judgmental, absorbed in past and future—often dominates, reinforcing a sense of separation. The right brain—intuitive, wordless, expansive—offers direct access to interbeing and presence. Both are needed; both are human. By cultivating mindfulness, we can quiet the left brain's restless grasping and invite the right brain's openness, even without the doorway of a stroke.

Dr. Taylor's story shows Nirvana is not a mystical realm far away. It is not an escape or an annihilation. It is a capacity within us—our right brain waiting patiently to be experienced. The Buddha spoke of Nirvana as "cooling," the end of grasping and aversion. Dr. Taylor's sudden immersion shows what happens when all that falls away: life, just as it is, boundless and whole.

This is not to romanticize illness or trauma. Dr. Taylor's recovery took years of hard, disciplined work. Yet her experience is a reminder: The spaciousness of Nirvana is not foreign to us. It is here, in every mindful breath and step, whenever we release the left brain's story of "me and mine" and rest in the right brain's vastness. To glimpse Nirvana does not require a stroke. It requires stopping, breathing, and touching the life that is already here—wordless, luminous, and boundless.

Refuge in Earth

Illness reminds us that this body cannot stand alone. It depends on countless conditions for its health and survival. When the body or mind becomes overwhelmed, one of the most reliable refuges is the earth itself. Long before modern medicine or technology, human beings instinctively turned toward the natural world for balance and healing. To place our feet on the ground, to feel the wind, to sit quietly beneath a tree—these simple gestures remind the body how to settle and return to itself.

Our planet Earth is profoundly beautiful. There's no other place we have discovered that offers such beauty and richness of life. How many young people nowadays take time to enjoy a sunrise or sunset, walk barefoot on the ground, or simply sit under a tree? How many adults still do this?

Whenever we have a moment of free time, many of us reach immediately for our phone or computer. We become absorbed in the virtual world while the body remains tense and the mind restless. Meanwhile, the subconscious continues processing everything we consume. When we finally return to the reality around us, it can feel even more overwhelming, and the impulse to escape again becomes stronger. It becomes a cycle of disconnection.

Yet true refuge cannot be found in escape. When we return to the earth—to the sky, the trees, the wind, the soil—we rediscover something very simple and very healing. Touching the earth's beauty and grace, moment after moment, nourishes the body and calms the mind. We remember how to be human again and how to connect with those around us. Nowadays, young people rarely have long conversations with their parents. Communication often happens through brief messages or online exchanges. While technology can be convenient, especially during times like the pandemic, it cannot replace genuine human presence.

Young people especially need opportunities to return to themselves and appreciate their youth, their health, and their many capacities. When so much energy is consumed by screens and games, only a narrow set of abilities develops while the rest of the mind and body remain undernourished. Adults must model another way of living. If we ourselves are constantly absorbed in media and entertainment, how can we guide young people toward balance?

When we remember to touch the earth, we remember something essential: This body is not separate from her. The air we breathe, the food we eat, and the ground beneath our feet are supporting our life. The Second Remembrance reminds us that this body is fragile and will not always function as we expect. Even in moments of illness or exhaustion, the earth continues to hold us with quiet patience. When we see clearly that our body is made of the earth, gratitude naturally arises. We begin to understand that caring for the earth is also caring for the conditions that support our own health and the well-being of future generations.

LIVE BEAUTIFULLY, DIE BEAUTIFULLY— TODAY

Caring for Body and Earth

Take a moment to sit up, perhaps rolling your shoulders a few times so they can open. Relax your arms. Offer your whole body a gentle smile. If you cannot sit, stand or lie down as you align the following phrases with your breath:

Hello, in-breath. Hello, out-breath. I know you're there. I'm so happy and grateful.

I can breathe easily without an oxygen mask, pain, or shortness of breath!

Breathing in, I cherish this in-breath.

Breathing out, I cherish this out-breath.

Breathing in, I use the ray of mindfulness to scan from the top of my head to the bottom of my feet.

Breathing out, I relax each part of my body.

Hello, precious body. You are made of the earth—of water, warmth, air, and soil.

Continue to follow your in-breath and out-breath as they are. Become aware of your body sitting on the ground or on a chair.

Breathing in, I feel my body sitting on the earth.

Breathing out, I feel the earth supporting me.

Hello, Mother Earth. You are truly a mother to us. Our flesh, the fluid in our body, and the heat in our body come from you. You give us shelter and daily sustenance. You hold us throughout our life, and when we die, you take us back.

Breathing in, I see that my body is made of the earth.
Breathing out, I feel gratitude for the earth.

Because our bodies come from earth and return to earth, the way we live our daily life also affects her health. When we forget this connection, we sometimes consume and act in ways that harm the very ground that sustains us. In the past, we may have lived in ways that harmed the earth without realizing it. Now, with awareness, we can live more simply and more lovingly.

Breathing in, I see that I am part of the earth.
Breathing out, I walk gently on this planet, choosing to live more simply and with care.

When I love and take care of myself through mindful consumption, simple living, and reaching out to help others, I can help you replenish and restore yourself so our children, grandchildren, and all future generations have a chance to live on this beautiful planet. When I touch the earth with awareness, my heart naturally opens. I remember the many beings that share this planet with me—humans, animals, plants, minerals, and future generations. I send well-wishes to those near and far who suffer from hunger, isolation, or sickness and those who must leave their country to find protection.

Breathing in, I touch the earth within me.
Breathing out, I care for the earth around me.

May I be safe. May I take care of my happiness in my breath, in my steps, in my positive, loving actions. Know that I matter, that my happiness matters to many. Everything I do matters, however small it is. When I brush my teeth, if I use a cup, I can save some water. I can always do something to help somebody, to preserve this planet. May I do everything out of love.

Breathing in, I take care of myself and my actions.
Breathing out, I act from love.

Soulmate to Myself

3

I am of
a nature
to die.
There is
no way to
escape
death.

One morning, I was walking toward the meditation hall for our morning meditation when a flower bud fell from an oleander branch. I had seen flowers fall many times before, but this time, as I walked peacefully and mindfully, the falling bud registered deeply in my mind. A flower doesn't have to be fully bloomed or withered in order to fall, I remembered. Even a bud—barely opened—can be shaken loose if a strong wind comes along. A flower can fall at any stage of its life. With deep awareness, though, the simple fact of life's inherent impermanence can be a transformative insight that changes how you look at yourself, how you view your circumstances, and how you respond to them—to life itself. Remembrance of our inevitable dying need not be a surrender to despair. It can be a reason to step more fully into the astonishing beauty of being here at all.

The Path Chose Me

I encountered death more than once in my young life—my mother disappeared when I was twelve, and my grandmother, who had held me through that loss, also passed away. Yet the full weight of impermanence did not reveal itself to me until the sudden death of someone I loved deeply.

Before becoming a nun, I was a young doctor who functioned well on the surface, even as depression and old wounds quietly shaped my days. One afternoon at the HIV clinic, an attending doctor casually mentioned a retreat Thầy would be leading in a few weeks. We had never spoken about Buddhism, yet he handed me a pamphlet that would change the course of my life. The decision to go seemed to make itself. I submitted a request for five days off, fully expecting it to be denied.

Instead, permission came the very next day. I went to Parallax Press, the Plum Village publishing house in Berkeley, to ask for financial assistance, and I was told I could help with tasks to reduce the cost. Everything fell into place as though it had been prearranged.

John drove me to the airport. Our relationship was strained—not because of anything he had done, but because my emotional landscape had grown dim. It was an old pattern of withdrawal I didn't yet understand. He had asked if he should join the retreat, but I told him I needed to go alone. "This retreat will decide the direction of my life," I said without fully understanding why.

At the retreat, I followed the schedule diligently. I had read *Peace Is Every Step,* one of Thầy's most popular books, on John's bookshelf, but I had never practiced meditation before. Listening to Thầy speak, his gentle presence reminded me of my grandmother. I cried through his Dharma talks. When Thầy taught the Four Noble Truths, I realized for the first time that although I had been a victim of abuse, I had also become a participant in my own suffering—through my thoughts, speech, and habitual ways of running and fighting. Wherever I went, there I was.

Walking meditation along the sea was breathtaking. On the first walk, I found myself behind Thầy. A thought flashed—"I can walk like him!"—a familiar impulse to measure myself against others. But the peace in his steps was its own teaching. My heart opened and I followed Thầy's footsteps with humility and gratitude. On the last day, I received the Five Mindfulness Trainings and the lineage name Joyful Service of the Heart.

When I returned home, my love for John resurfaced clearly and tenderly. Yet I also felt bound by the Third Mindfulness Training, which asks us to be utterly certain of long-term commitment before engaging in sexual intimacy. I told John I could not share the same bed and moved my pillow to the couch. He was confused and hurt. The gulf between us widened, and my old habits—rigidity, righteousness, depression—rushed in to fill it. Within two weeks, despite all I had learned, I was once again slipping away from myself and into depression.

My birthday was approaching. John wanted us to celebrate, but I told him I was on call the night before and unsure if I could see him. As I drove to Oakland through golden sunlight and crisp air that morning, I felt our love again and promised myself I'd see him the next day. When I reached Oakland, thick fog swallowed everything. It struck me that life was like this too: suddenly unclear, even though the sun still shone somewhere above the clouds.

That night in the emergency room, my pager went off. It was my best friend, Jennifer. The moment I heard her voice, I knew. She told me John had gone swimming at Half Moon Bay and never came back. His clothes were on the beach, and his car remained in the parking lot. The Coast Guard had searched but found nothing.

I drove to the ocean, calling for John, weeping, howling into the dark. The waves crashed hard. I felt impossibly small. All I could do was pray. In my heart, I knew I would not see him again.

On the drive home, I told Jennifer, "I'm not going back to medicine." Something in me had broken open. I saw clearly that no amount of success or love could fill the cavern of unresolved suffering inside me. My grandmother's old wish for me to become a nun—a wish I had long dismissed—surfaced with startling clarity. I realized it might be the only path left other than death.

When I arrived back at the apartment, it felt warm and tender, as if John had left a final blessing. He had done the laundry and folded my clothes. I lit incense and knelt before the altar with photos of Avalokitesvara, the bodhisattva of compassion; my grandmother; and my mother. My mind was strangely calm. When the incense burned out, I stood and looked out over the city. Morning sunlight reflected off windows in the distance, forming a giant anatomical heart. I cried out, "I see you, John!"

We returned to the beach the next morning—my birthday. A foil balloon drifted across the water and landed near me. It read "Happy Birthday," as if John had sent a final message.

His mother and sister came soon after. I asked for nothing but his poncho and sleeping bag. When I finally slept, I dreamed of floating on a vast, silent ocean—peaceful and infinite. I felt certain John had let go peacefully too. He had always said he wished to die at sea.

Finding the Way Home

In the two months after John's death, I began preparing to leave for Plum Village. I gave away almost everything I owned. Those weeks felt like walking through a corridor between two lives. I slept on the floor of the bare apartment, wrapped in John's sleeping bag. I wasn't afraid of ghosts—I felt like a ghost myself. Grief hollowed me, emptied me, and I moved through the days as though my body kept living while my spirit lagged far behind.

For days the despair was so strong I drove along Highway 1, staring at the cliffs and the crashing waves below. How beautiful and full of promise that road had once seemed to us, the many times John and I explored its sweeping vistas and hidden beaches. Now, all I saw were the places where everything could end in an instant if I just turned the steering wheel a few inches. And yet something in me held. I couldn't bear the thought of my brother finding out I had given up. So instead of driving off the edge, I would turn around, return to the apartment, curl into John's sleeping bag, and cry until morning. I could never remember if I had eaten. Raw despair was my fuel.

One morning, I drove to the hospital to resign from my medical residency. The hospital administrators and my colleagues were empathetic and kind, though they did not understand. One asked, "Will you really shave off your beautiful hair?" Another asked, "What if you realize you made the wrong decision?" I said I would give monastic life five years, but inside I knew: This wasn't a career change. This was self-preservation.

Life became strangely perilous during that time. Strangers sensed my vulnerability—some with kindness, others with predatory certainty. I found myself in situations that could have ended disastrously. A man drove me down a deserted road; a mechanic tried to pressure me into going away with him; colleagues professed their love for me. Each time, some small current—courage, intuition, protection—carried me through and kept me steady. All I wanted was true peace.

Eventually, the only thing left was to leave. My brother Sonny flew to San Francisco to be with me on the forty-ninth day after John's passing, a day on which Buddhist ceremonies would be performed for him. Unable to accept my decision to become a nun, Sonny sat alone in his car outside the temple during John's ceremonies. Although we had lost our parents young, I had always been a stable presence for my brother. Now he feared he was losing me, too.

I carried only what I could fit into a backpack: a few sets of clothes, John's sleeping bag and poncho, the pair of Teva sandals he had given me as his first gift. When I arrived in Plum Village, I was raw and jagged with grief, stripped of direction. The quiet there was unsettling and consoling at the same time. The monks and nuns walked slowly, each step placed carefully on the earth. I wrote a letter to Thầy asking to become a nun, pouring everything onto the page—my despair, my near-suicidal drives along Highway 1, the nights wrapped in John's sleeping bag, the hollow ache of losing every plan I had made for my life. Most of all, I wrote that I no longer knew how to live.

Thầy did not answer with advice or explanations, but with his presence: the way he drank his tea, the way he smiled. The way the Sangha breathed together in silence. It was as if the whole community whispered: "You are safe now. Stay. Breathe!" Little by little, my breath returned. Not without tears, but just one moment after the next.

Learning to Die Daily

John's death opened a door in me that I could not, would not, close again. Once I arrived at Plum Village, Thầy began teaching me how to look directly at death, not with despair, but with clarity. What I learned there has shaped every day of my life since.

To face death is not only to face the moment the body stops breathing. It is to face the truth of impermanence in each breath, each step, each letting go. Learning to die daily is how we learn to live fully. Through practice we begin to see nothing can be grasped—not our bodies, not our thoughts, not the people we love. When we accept this, we live with a different kind of tenderness, no longer sacrificing our health to make excess money and then sacrificing our money to recuperate our health. When we see death, we see what a waste it is to be so anxious about the future that we can't enjoy the present. If we stop living as if we will never die, then we will not die without having lived.

One way I practice dying each day is very simple: I keep my space in order. I place the lid back on my cup. I tidy my room and make my bed. Before traveling, I sort through my belongings to see what can be given away. Monastics do this before each three-month winter Rains Retreat. These small acts remind me nothing truly belongs to me; I could leave this body at any moment. When I go to sleep, I expect to wake—but I also know I might not. When I travel, I may or may not return. This awareness is not morbid. It is freeing.

The Buddha taught that among all wholesome deeds, the greatest merit comes from the simple awareness of impermanence. Everything changes. Our joys, our sorrows, our youth, our strength—none of it stays. The earth itself is impermanent. When we forget this, we cling to what has already passed or chase after what has not yet come. When we remember impermanence, we stop waiting for life to begin. We recognize what is available to us right now: our breath, our health, our relationships, our community, our capacity to practice. Gratitude becomes a wellspring of energy and joy.

Many of us focus on our views and ambitions and forget to care for our bodies and minds. When life does not unfold the way we imagined, we collapse into despair and thoughts of worthlessness. We spend so much time fighting outward battles that when we finally turn inward, we feel estranged from ourselves. This is why daily practice matters.

With each breath, we touch the truth of life and death: To breathe in, we must release the out-breath; to breathe out, we must release the in-breath. Each breath is a small life and death. Mindfulness becomes a rehearsal for dying with dignity and without fear—a practice of letting go, of loosening our grasp, of opening the heart. In Buddhism, death is not simply the cessation of respiration. It is also the closing in of craving, fear, or despair. Death, in this deeper sense, is not only the end of the body. It is any moment when we lose the capacity to see clearly, to love, to be kind. Wrong views like craving, fear, and hatred are all forms of dying. Awareness, presence, and understanding are forms of birth.

The Buddha once described people as being like "fresh young grass, cut and laid out in the sun to dry"—bright with potential, yet quickly withering when caught in regret for the past, fear of the future, and distraction in the present. Not long ago, a young man, strong and full of life, told me, "I feel like I am dying. I can't live my life. I'm full of anxiety and unable to do anything!" He was like that fresh young grass—vibrant in form, yet already losing life because he was consumed by fear, longing, and restlessness. If you ever feel dimmed by a sense of bleakness or disconnection, try visualizing yourself as that young grass, freshly cut and laid out to dry. See how quickly life slips away when we are not rooted in the present moment. Then breathe, and gently return.

The flower does not stop being when it withers. It becomes fragrance, compost, soil, nourishment for new seeds. When we look deeply, we see dying is not separate from living. It is another form of continuation. To live fully, we must learn to die in each moment—to let go of what no longer serves us, to soften our fixed ideas, to release our grasp on the people we love. Then life becomes real. Precious. Possible.

The Non-Fear of Nirvana

To understand why we fear dying, we must first understand why we cling so tightly to the idea of a separate "me" who can disappear. Through daily practice we begin to accept impermanence with the heart. But to truly touch non-fear, we must also understand how the mind creates the illusion of a separate self that can be destroyed.

Our brain is composed of two hemispheres: the left and the right. Modern society tends to favor the left hemisphere, which emphasizes language, analytical thinking, categorization, boundaries, and limitations. It is the voice that constantly speaks in terms of "I, me, my, myself, and mine" and easily creates a sense of separation and isolation. It keeps score, compares, measures, calculates, judges. It creates the sense of a separate self that must defend itself at all costs—even when no danger is present. Its function is to sort, label, and distinguish. But when overused, it can reinforce the illusion that we are fundamentally separate from one another. When this way of seeing dominates our experience, death appears terrifying. If I am a separate self enclosed in this body, then death looks like total annihilation.

Within us also lies the right hemisphere, which experiences life in a very different way. It is expansive, interconnected, and attuned to oneness. It senses life directly, without commentary. It knows belonging without needing proof. It doesn't ask, "Who am I compared to you?" It simply experiences that we inter-are. It is quiet, capacious, unconcerned with labels or hierarchies. It perceives life directly, without concepts. This is the part of us capable of touching Nirvana—not as a distant spiritual realm but as a lived experience of non-fear and interbeing.

In the practice of mindful breathing, we focus on our in-breath and out-breath, gently relaxing and quieting the mind. Over time, our sense of separation softens. We feel more at ease and more connected to what is inside of and around us. There is no longer such a strong sense of a separate breather. There is only the breath, only the act of breathing. The right hemisphere can sense this fluid, dynamic, and interconnected way of being.

Mindful breathing—and in fact, all mindfulness practices—help quiet the analytical mind and open a wider field of awareness. Zen practice cultivates our capacity to simply *be*—free from inner chatter and rigid boundaries. In that space, the walls between "you" and "me"—on individual as well as community levels—begin to shrink. When we dwell in spacious awareness, we touch *suchness*—the simple, profound reality of things as they are. There is no birth and no death, only continuous transformation. This is a glimpse of Nirvana available in each mindful breath.

This experience is available to us in our daily lives if we allow ourselves the time and space to quiet the mind. This can mean refraining from turning to electronic devices to check our messages, the news, or social media as soon as we have a spare moment. Constant stimulation of this kind keeps the analytical mind constantly activated and can make us feel increasingly alienated and disconnected from ourselves, our families, society, other species, and the earth. When we become absorbed in ourselves—isolated in our own fears, desires, and needs—we risk falling into patterns of greed and selfishness. *Just me: my safety, my comfort, my suffering, my needs, my desires.* The more entangled we are in self-centered thinking, the more miserable we feel. We never feel safe enough. Never happy enough. Never have enough. Never *are* enough. This is samsara in neurological form—circling in our own fear-based narratives. When we engage more with openness, intuition, and connection, we begin to access the deeper truth of who we are. We touch the boundless peace and joy that dwell within us.

When we touch this deeper way of perceiving, fear of death begins to soften. We no longer see life as something confined to a single body or a single lifetime. When a fire burns through the night, its embers cool by morning. In the ancient world, that coolness was called *nirvana*. The fire has not been destroyed—it has simply gone out, returning to stillness. Nirvana does not extinguish life; it extinguishes wrong perceptions. Nirvana is what remains when fear and illusions of separation no longer dominate our experience. It is not a destination beyond this life, but a state of peace in the midst of it. It is the cooling of the fires of craving, fear, and grasping. We touch Nirvana each time we release our need to control, each time we rest in what is. The doorway to Nirvana—not as a metaphysical realm, but as a quality of consciousness—is available in each breath. Nirvana is non-fear. Nirvana is our true nature.

Living and Dying Are Not Two

The more I practiced living with impermanence—keeping my space simple, touching gratitude each day, breathing with the truth that nothing is guaranteed—the more another understanding slowly revealed itself. Death was not separate from life. It was holding my hand all along, guiding me toward a clearer way of living.

When the Buddha was still a young teacher, a group of students came to him full of questions about how to live happily and keep the vitality of youth from slipping away. In response, he offered a simple but radical truth, later known as The Discourse on Youth and Happiness. True happiness, he told them, cannot be found in possessions, reputation, or sensory pleasure. These shimmer and fade like dew in the morning sun. Lasting joy arises from understanding the nature of things, from seeing clearly that all phenomena are impermanent and nothing we love can be held onto forever. When we understand this, we stop grasping. We begin to live with gratitude instead of fear.

Among the Buddha's young disciples, there was one who understood this teaching deeply. When a goddess questioned him about why he had turned away from pleasures of the senses, he answered in a way that has guided generations of practitioners: "I have not abandoned the present moment to chase after pleasures in a distant future," he told her. "I have given up untimely pleasures for the deepest happiness of this moment." When she pressed him to explain, he said, "The Buddha taught that in sensual desire is little sweetness and much bitterness, small benefit and great danger. Now, dwelling in the Dharma here and now, I have given up the burning fire of afflictions."[8]

The Dharma is not far away. It is this very breath. When we return to our breathing—the moment the phone rings, when restlessness arises—we are dwelling in the Dharma. Peace is available now, not after we fix our lives, not after we achieve some imagined future. As the Buddha said, "The Dharma always invites us to come and see."[9]

When we live unmindfully, craving burns within us. Desire feeds on itself. A young man watching pornography on an airplane at sunrise (something I once witnessed) is not an evil person—he is simply caught in the flames of habit energy, seeking comfort in a place that can never satisfy. We all know this fire in our own ways. These are the five sensual desires—sex, wealth, fame, food, and sleep. Each promises satisfaction, yet each, when clung to, becomes a path toward suffering.

Zen teachings say that when we do not know the true nature of desire, we proceed on the path to death. Each time we lose ourselves in craving, we step away from the living present. Each time we come back to our breath, we return to life. To live in awareness is to live in harmony with death as a teacher, a beloved companion. Each breath arises and dissolves. Each thought is born and dies. Every relationship, every season, carries arrival and departure. The practice is not to resist this movement but to live within it. We bow to life's unfolding without demanding it last forever. Understanding this, the Buddha's young disciples began to experience freedom—not through the promise of eternal youth, but through intimacy with change. When we know nothing lasts, we also know nothing is ever truly lost. What we love continues in new forms—a cloud becomes rain, a river, mist.

When we look deeply, we see that nothing truly begins and nothing truly ends. Thầy often taught, "Nothing is born, nothing dies. There is only continuation." Our parents and ancestors are alive in us—not as memory alone, but as breath, heartbeat, and consciousness. The air, the soil, the sun, and the food we eat are present in each of our cells. Where could we go when we "die"? Into what could we possibly vanish?

One day my niece asked my brother and me in great seriousness, "Would you rather eat ice cream that tastes like poop, or poop that tastes like ice cream?" My brother chose the latter; I chose the former. We laughed, but it later struck me how often we frame life inside those narrow choices—either this or that, either yes or no—without recognizing the spaciousness of reality. The Buddha called this the trap of views. We suffer not because reality is cruel but because we confine it within small conceptual boxes: being/not being, birth/death, coming/going. These dualities are lines drawn in water. They are convenient illusions that undermine our humanity.

When I sit beside someone who is dying, I don't see an ending. I see a doorway, a returning. Each out-breath is already a small death; each in-breath, a small birth. When we breathe with awareness of coming and going as one motion, we are free. This understanding doesn't erase grief, but it removes despair. We still mourn, but with tenderness rather than terror. We still love, but without fear. Life becomes precious because it is fleeting. We treasure the ordinary—the warmth of a cup in our hands, the laughter of a niece, the scent of rain. The present moment becomes enough.

To live beautifully is to die beautifully—not someday, but breath by breath. Each moment of understanding is a preparation for death. Each moment of letting go is a small liberation. Living and dying inter-are. They are one continuous movement, endlessly taking shape and dissolving again. When we touch this, we touch freedom. Breathing in, we know this moment is alive. Breathing out, we release our fear of losing it.

Life is here.

Death is here.

They are not two.

LIVE BEAUTIFULLY, DIE BEAUTIFULLY— TODAY

Write Your Own Living Will

In our society, conversations about dying are often avoided until it is too late. Yet preparing for death is also preparing for reconciliation and peace. Writing a living will is not an act of despair, but of clarity and compassion. It allows those who care for us to understand our deepest wishes and to support us to die in alignment with our values.

When we write our living will, we affirm trust in the natural course of life and death. We acknowledge impermanence not as an enemy, but as a companion. The following is my own living will, written during a time of health and lucidity. I offer it here as encouragement for you to look deeply into your own values, to face what is inevitable with calm understanding, and to write down your wishes in the spirit of mindfulness. A living will is not only a medical instruction; it is also a mirror of our deepest understanding of life and death.

September 17, 2016

Sister Dang Nghiem's Living Will

My beloved monastic siblings and my brother Sonny,

I am writing this letter in my clearest state of mind. Please help me make these sound choices and decisions when I cannot do so for myself.

At this point, I feel I have lived my life fully. I experienced some joy and a lot of suffering growing up. Thanks to my monastic practice, I now experience much more joy than suffering. I feel I can let go of this life at any moment. I do not want to hold on to life for the sake of quantity, for the sake of more time at any cost.

Therefore, if something were to happen to me, be it an accident or a terminal illness, I would like my body to follow its natural course without too much medical intervention:

I would like NOT to be resuscitated—DNR (Do Not Resuscitate).

I would like NOT to be intubated.

I would like NOT to be kept alive for more than three days if I were in a coma.

I would like NOT to be fed with a gastric or nasogastric feeding tube. If I cannot eat by mouth, let me fast and let my body shut down naturally.

If my cognitive and/or physical functions are greatly impaired, please advocate euthanasia for me.

I would like some pain medication if the pain were intense, but not so much that my awareness is fogged.

I would like to be brought back to the monastery to pass away there instead of in the hospital and to be cremated in a simple cardboard coffin.

Please do not perform an autopsy on me for any reason.

Most of all, I wish to be fully aware of my surroundings and my breath, all the way to my last moment. I no longer expect someone special to be at my side during my final moments. I trust that whoever can be there for me will do so with kindness and respect, and that is enough for me.

The person I've loved most unconditionally and for the longest time is my brother Sonny. I spent many years fearing his loneliness and his death. Now, he has his daughter Sunee, with whom he shares a deep and immeasurable love, and I can rest in peace, without regret or worry for him.

At this stage in my life, ambitions and glories are no longer as important as the wish to become kinder, gentler, and more accepting of others. I have learned to love and care for many people, and I have received an abundance of love and support in return. Please forgive my shortcomings, just as I forgive yours. All is well.

I wish to be aware of the coming of my death within days or weeks. My affairs are in order, I have nothing to regret, my mind is clear, and my body is at ease. In my final moments, I hope not to wait for anyone or anything. I hold no regrets, sorrow, or longing. I am doing my best in my daily practice to love myself and to let go.

This part of the discourse "Turning to the Tathagata"[10] *reflects the deep wish for my own departure:*

> *I pray that my body and mind are peaceful and happy,*
> *free and at ease the moment I leave this life,*
> *my heart with no regrets, body without pain,*
> *thoughts unclouded by ignorance,*
> *my mindfulness clear and bright,*
> *and six senses as calm as*
> *when I enter meditative concentration.*

—Living will signed by Sister Dang Nghiem

After reading these words, pause for a moment. Let them settle in your heart. A living will is not only something to read, but something to contemplate in the light of your own life.

When you feel ready, you may wish to write your own living will in the same spirit of clarity and mindfulness. After you complete your own living will, take a few breaths to read it aloud—to yourself, to a loved one, or simply into the silence of the room. This is not only a legal document; it is a spiritual practice. It helps you touch your own freedom, knowing you have faced humanity's deepest fear.

Such preparation is an act of compassion for yourself and for those who will care for you. To live beautifully includes dying beautifully, with understanding and equanimity. When we face death directly, life reveals itself more vividly—each breath, each moment a precious continuation.

Take a gentle breath now, and feel the gift of being alive in this moment.

Not Leaving Myself

A wealthy man once offered a large donation to a temple and asked the Zen Master to write a calligraphy for his home. The Zen Master wrote: "Grandfather dies. Children die. Grandchildren die." Horrified, the man thought he was being cursed. Calmly, the Zen Master explained, "When the young die before the old, it is a great misfortune, a deep sorrow. It is a blessing when the elderly live to see the younger generations outlive them." While the Zen Master's words are profound, most people tend to take this natural cycle for granted.

For many of us, suffering arrives early and unexpectedly, rearranging the shape of our lives long before we are ready. For me, the wish to disappear first manifested when I was a child. I didn't have the language to call it despair or trauma. I only knew the feeling of wanting the pain to stop. Since I was nine years old, riding my bicycle across a bridge, I wondered what it would be like to plunge into the river below. At fifteen, triggered by the uncle who had molested me in the past, I swallowed an entire bottle of pain pills, sat down on the wooden plank bed, and waited to die.

Nothing happened. Yet that day (with what turned out to be expired medication) remains vivid in me because it was the first time I made a decisive move to end my life. I crossed an invisible threshold, and a pattern opened in my mind that would return again and again in my teens and young adulthood. Whenever life became overwhelming—especially in romantic relationships—the idea of disappearing arose automatically, almost mechanically. It was not always a genuine intention to die. Sometimes it was simply habit, the mind reaching for the only exit it knew. Thoughts rehearsed over years grow their own roots.

When life feels unbearable, when we do not yet know how to stay with ourselves, the practice can show us another way. Long before I found Zen practice, I had tried to escape my despair by changing cities, countries, even partners—but everywhere I went, the same heaviness followed. I simply didn't know how to stay with myself.

Suicide happens in many families. Often, it is not because we truly hate life, but because our suffering feels endless and we see no other way out. At nine, fifteen, nineteen, I did not have the language for trauma or depression. I only knew the conviction: *This will never change. I cannot bear it.*

Looking back as a practitioner, I see how early suicidal thoughts became habit energy and then my personality. When John drowned, that old reflex came back with full force. I could not imagine returning to medicine or to any kind of "normal life." In truth, it was not life I wanted to end, but the weight of my grief. I felt as if I were far from shore, treading cold water in a vast, dark ocean. "Why should I struggle any longer?" my despair whispered. "What is the point?"

If I had not met Thầy at a mindfulness retreat three weeks before John's death, I might have followed that voice. At the retreat, I had encountered the Four Noble Truths as a mirror that showed me my suffering was not mine alone; suffering is a human condition. I saw that there are "nutriments" that feed our suffering and that I had fed my own despair and suicidal thoughts for many years, long after the abuse and losses had passed. I had become, without knowing it, the perpetrator of my own misery.

The third and fourth Noble Truths were my lifeline: Suffering can be transformed, and there is a path. That simple possibility gave me just enough faith to step away from the edge and toward practice. Modern medicine had many tools, but none could take away the anguish that flooded me. What I longed for was true peace. The path became my only way forward. Leaving medicine to ordain as a nun in France was not a rejection of life; it was my deepest attempt to stay alive.

As a nun, I began to investigate the roots of my suffering—not only the external causes, but also the inner mindscape of my thoughts, speech, and actions. As children, we are often helpless in the face of violence or neglect. We develop survival strategies: fighting back, running away, or freezing. One of my strategies was to fantasize about death. Since my teenage years, I believed I would die at twenty-six. Giving myself that deadline made life strangely bearable; I trusted it would all end soon anyway.

Thoughts, like seeds, do not stay still. Think of an oak tree producing millions of acorns. Each acorn can become another tree, producing millions more. In the same way, our thoughts give rise to more thoughts, words, and behaviors that reinforce our patterns. A child who feels helpless and hopeless often grows into an adult who struggles to trust others and themselves. Unless we learn another way, we continue to abandon ourselves.

Over the last twenty-five years as a nun, I have discovered three inner powers that have helped me learn not to leave myself: the power of understanding, the power of love, and the power of transformation and healing. Thanks to these powers, suicidal thoughts rarely visit now. When they do appear, they are like the shadow of an old friend. I can smile and say, "Hello, I see you," and let them pass. I no longer need to wish for death, because I see that I am already dying and being reborn in each moment. My deepest wish now is simply to live beautifully and to die beautifully, one breath at a time.

The first power, the power of understanding, comes from daily mindfulness. I learn from my own breath. Throughout the day, my breath faithfully reflects the state of my mind—angry or calm, anxious or at ease. When I notice my breathing is tight, hurried, heavy, or uneven, I stop. I stand still, or sit, or lie down. I place my hands on my belly and feel its gentle rise and fall. If my breathing is very shallow, I simply feel the air in my nostrils or on my lips. Silently, I tell myself, "I'm here for you. I love you. I won't abandon you. I won't hurt you." From this understanding grows the second power, the power of love. In recent years, I have written many calligraphies: *"Safe in myself, safe in the world," "At ease in myself, at ease in the world," "I am beautiful. I am whole."* These are not slogans; they are insights earned through many moments of coming home to my body and feelings. When violent thoughts arise, instead of acting them out or pushing them away, I return to my breath and my steps. I walk slowly and gently. I speak to myself with kindness: "This will pass. I won't run away. I won't neglect you. I won't hurt you, even in my thoughts."

Little by little, this simple act has made me safe to myself. When we are at ease and safe within, we can feel at ease and safe wherever we go in the world.

Mindfulness also strengthens the third power: the power of transformation and healing. Our skin cells are changing every moment; thoughts and feelings rise and fall like currents in a river. It is our unexamined views that keep regenerating suffering, the way an oak tree produces endless acorns. When we practice seeing impermanence in the body, in our emotions, in the people and situations around us, something breaks open. We realize: This pain is not fixed. This story is not the whole of who I am.

One of the deepest insights that has kept me alive is interbeing. Interbeing means this is in that and that is in this. In a beautiful orchid, there are non-orchid elements: sunshine, rain, soil, the gardener, the truck driver, the florist, the hopes and skills of many generations. The orchid is there because of countless causes and conditions. When it is no longer on the table, it has not truly vanished. Certain conditions have simply changed.

Sometimes, the pain runs too deep or the patterns are too strong for us to save ourselves. At times, we can hold on for someone we love. Interbeing helped me stay when the thought of suicide felt strongest. One of the reasons I did not end my life before I ordained was my younger brother Sonny. Whenever I imagined dying, I saw him left completely alone in the world: no parents, no relatives, no sister. I understood that no matter how much I loved him, that love would not protect him from despair if I abandoned him. In the same way, he has told me there were times he held a gun to his own temple and thought of me. The thought of leaving me alone stopped him. My brother and I saved our own lives and each other's lives with the insight of interbeing long before we knew the word.

There is no real beginning or end, no fixed birth or death—only transmission and reception. If we do not transform what we have received, we will pass it on. If we do transform it, that healing is also transmitted. Seeing this clearly, I made a vow: to transform my sadness, despair, and suffering so I may transmit understanding, peace, and acceptance to my brother and to many others. This is something I can do. Each moment I breathe mindfully, I remember: "I will not leave myself." This is how I have learned, in a very concrete way, to live beautifully and to die beautifully in each moment.

About Coming and Going

After I began learning not to leave myself, the next step on the path was discovering I didn't have to walk alone. Thầy's presence—steady, simple, and deeply human—became a refuge I could rely on when my own mind felt unsafe. His teachings reached me not through philosophy, but through ordinary moments that revealed how I could train my mind to stay, to breathe, to see clearly. These small lessons became the anchors that kept me from slipping back into the old abyss.

I had actually encountered Thầy long before we met. After my mother disappeared, when I was still a child wandering temple grounds with sadness and pain too big for my small body, I had found a poem pinned to a bulletin board. I read it only once, but something in its sorrow and tenderness sank into me. For years I sang it softly as I walked—my own improvised tune to words I felt completely. After I became a nun, during the Rose Ceremony for honoring our parents, I realized with a start: The poem had been written by Thầy! He had touched my life without either of us knowing it.

One stanza I had carried since childhood echoed inside me again:

Twilight draped the grave,
temple bells softly tolling.
I realized that losing my mother
was losing the whole sky.

After I became a nun, Thầy guided me again, revealing how to live and die with dignity, tenderness, and peace. In his presence, I began to see what John had shown me too: To love life is to accept its impermanence. The two cannot be separated. Their lives—one a teacher, one a beloved partner—became mirrors showing me the same truth: When we live mindfully, we can die beautifully. Understanding death, we learn how to truly live.

In 2001, Thầy went to the US for a teaching tour. I had been ordained less than a year, so I remained at Plum Village. At the airport security checkpoint, as luggage was passing through the scanner, Thầy pointed and said to me, "You see, my child? It goes in one end and comes out the other. Life and death are like that too. Nothing is lost!"

His words were so simple—visual, concrete. Standing there beside him, the image imprinted itself in me even though I did not yet fully understand it. It helped me begin to see life and death as movement rather than disappearance. We see a form, then we don't—but nothing has actually vanished. It simply manifests elsewhere.

After Thầy had checked in, he waved me close. Speaking through the space between two panels of glass, he said, "While you are staying at home, enjoy doing walking meditation for Thầy."

At that time, returning to my breath or my steps felt almost impossible. A whole day might pass without me being aware of a single step. After Thầy's encouragement, I began to try harder. I made a quiet contract with myself: to walk mindfully from my room to the dining hall. Sometimes I was present for a few steps, then forgot the rest. Sometimes I'd turn around and try again, only to lose attention after a few more steps. My mind drifted constantly to the past, to sorrowful thoughts, until I'd find myself swept away. I kept trying to anchor my mind in my breath and my steps so it wouldn't keep dragging me off and under, and gradually the practice began to calm me. Every time I saw Thầy, or my monastic brothers and sisters walking mindfully, I remembered: return to your steps.

A year later, I would recognize that same teaching again—not at an airport, but while walking behind Thầy in meditation. One day, I climbed a magnolia tree right in front of Thầy's room while staying next to his hermitage for a week with a group of sisters. Seeing parasitic plants growing on it, I spent hours pulling them off and throwing them to the ground. Restlessness had always been my survival instinct, and here it was again, trying to fix everything.

That evening, we had a meal with Thầy. While everyone ate quietly and peacefully, tears fell into my bowl; I couldn't eat. After dinner, Thầy called me, "Follow me, my child." We went to the small meditation room next to the kitchen. Thầy began to walk slowly, signaling me to walk with him. The thick carpet beneath our feet recorded each step. Thầy circled slowly in walking meditation, and I followed behind him. After a while, I realized I couldn't tell which footsteps were his and which were mine. I couldn't tell where the steps began or ended. For the first time, I felt myself moving in harmony with something larger than my own wounded life. Those mindful footsteps taught me not to see my suffering as isolated, but as part of a larger continuity involving my family, my ancestors, and all of humanity. What I carried was never mine alone. What I healed would never be mine alone either. We often try to assert ourselves as individuals, to leave our imprint. Yet the practice revealed something else: My steps were never only my steps. My life was interwoven with countless lives. While we each have this one life, we must also do our best to live beautifully, to live harmoniously with ourselves and with each other. This is our one chance to do our best in these endless circles.

I experienced this insight again at Central Park in New York recently. People streamed through the park from every entrance—young and old, fast and slow, dressed in every possible way. No single person defined the movement. Yet together they formed a continuous flow of life.

As I remembered walking behind Thầy more than twenty years earlier, I saw how each of us is only a small part of this vast current of humanity, and yet each step still matters. Each of us carries suffering. Each of us carries the possibility of understanding. We are each responsible for learning to be a soulmate to our own suffering, to our own trauma, to each other's suffering, and to each other's trauma. If we can just do that, then our life is meaningful and worthwhile. Even if we were to die tonight, we could be at peace—because we have made peace with ourselves and with our life; with those who have hurt us and those whom we have hurt; with what was, what is, and what will be.

Learning to make peace begins with every breath and with every step. Make peace in your own body. Make peace with your left foot, with your right foot, one step at a time. Make peace with your own feelings. When we learn to walk this way, something very simple becomes clear: We were never walking alone.

When the Ground Moves

Recently, an earthquake of magnitude 5.2 struck San Diego County, home of Deer Park Monastery. That evening, during our Happiness Meeting, one monastic sister described what happened as the tremors began. She had been just outside the meditation hall.

"There was nowhere to run!" she said. "I couldn't go back into the hall, and I couldn't just sit down on the ground. So, I tried to do walking meditation." It was an unnerving experience, and even as she described it, a trace of the fear lingered in her voice. A lay woman shared next, "To be honest, I wasn't afraid. I was with another lay friend, so I put my hand on her shoulder and asked if she was okay." She paused. "Maybe I should check in with myself more. That's what I'm learning here. To be honest, I'm not afraid of death. Living is much more difficult for me!"

Earthquakes reveal something we usually forget: There is no solid ground to depend on—neither beneath our feet nor in our lives. In those moments, our true refuge is not outside us. It is the quality of presence we offer to ourselves and to one another. When the ground moves, mindfulness becomes the only place we can stand.

Caring for the Sick and Dying

When someone we love becomes seriously ill or begins to die, the truth of the Third Remembrance appears directly in our lives. It forces us to confront our own mortality, which can be terrifying. We may also harbor feelings of resentment toward our loved ones: "You're going to leave me. You're going to abandon me if you're sick and dying like this." In this state, we feel threatened in every way. Trapped in this mindset, we struggle to offer the love, attention, care, and support that our loved ones desperately need—and that we genuinely want to give.

Instead, we might distance ourselves, building a wall to protect our hearts, unknowingly missing the chance to truly be there for our beloved, to heal our relationship with them, and to cultivate a life free from fear. In spiritual practice, we learn to confront birth and death more directly, often through the Five Remembrances, touching both our mortality and immortality right within us. This allows us to stay grounded and present when a loved one is sick or dying, ready to offer the care they need, even when they are still in denial or unable to receive it with grace.

We learn to deeply understand and connect with those we love—understanding not only their suffering but also their dreams and aspirations. To truly know our parents is to understand ourselves, because we carry their dreams, their pain, and even their unresolved issues within us.

Even if our parents have passed, it's never too late. They continue to live inside us. My mother passed away when I was only twelve, yet through my spiritual practice, I've learned more about her than I could have ever known in life.

In my early thirties, I began to experience joint and muscle pain that left me frustrated and irritated. One day, during meditation, an image of my mother in her early thirties surfaced—she, too, had suffered from similar pain. I remembered how she would ask my brother and me to walk on her back to relieve some of it. This was a profound revelation: My mother's pain was now manifesting in my own body! From that moment on, I felt a deep, visceral connection to my mother—both emotionally and physically—and to the pain she had once endured. It gave me the strength to accept and bear my own pain with greater grace and willingness.

Artificial Immortality

Questions such as "Can we avoid death?" or "Can death be optional?" have been asked for millennia. Today, many in the scientific, medical, and technological communities are searching for ways to make death optional—or at least delayable.

One of the newest proposals is what some call "artificial immortality." This is the idea that if we cannot keep the body alive forever, perhaps we can preserve a digital version of the person. The underlying assumption is that consciousness can be reduced to data. If consciousness is just data, the contents of a person's life can theoretically be transferred to a supercomputer, known as a "mind file," to be stored indefinitely.

If you want a mind file, you provide a company with as many photos of yourself as possible, record all the significant events of your life, and share how you felt about them. A digital version of you is created from these materials for your children to continue "interacting" with, receiving algorithmic responses after you die. For example, your child might ask your digital version, "Mom, what did you feel when you gave birth to me?" The supercomputer will search your mind file, locate a photo, and infer your emotional state from your facial expression. If the software detects 90 percent happiness and 10 percent relief, your avatar might answer, "I felt very happy and relieved when I gave birth to you." Such neat responses hide the complexity of real experience—what happened before, after, and beneath the moment the camera captured.

There are already prototypes, such as a digital version of Deepak Chopra, which people can question about meditation or personal challenges. These mind files offer a comforting illusion, a "me" that seems to continue. It is easy to understand the longing behind these efforts. Human beings have always searched for ways to extend life, preserve memory, and remain present for those we love. But from the perspective of interbeing, we have never been a single, isolated self to preserve. Even as technology tries to outsmart death, the deepest continuation we leave behind is still our actions, our healing, our understanding, and our love.

A Good Death

The past is both gone and living on in this very moment. Our worldview, the way we see ourselves, and the way we think, speak, and behave are all shaped by the past. Since the past continues in us, we also have the chance—right now—to tend to what remains unfinished or unresolved.

People may consider thinking about death to be morbid and assume there is no such thing as a good death. Yet I've discovered a good death can be a great offering to ourselves and those we love.

I no longer yearn for fame, wealth, or romance. What I wish for, deeply, is a good death. I've come to see that to die well is to live each moment with beauty and presence. A good death does not happen in the future—it's something we practice now, by dying beautifully in each moment.

Tend to negative thoughts and unresolved conflicts. Hold them gently, understand them, and let them go. That is dying beautifully. That is living deeply. If we can do it today, we can do it tomorrow, and every day, right up to our final breath. A good death is simply the continuation of a good life lived with clarity and kindness, nothing left tangled or unspoken in our hearts.

This morning, while lying in bed and gently massaging my body, a thought arose: I'm aware that you are growing old, becoming ill, and dying, and I'm grateful for your bravery and persistent efforts. Aware of your impermanence, I'm grateful for your enduring loyalty. Aware of your vulnerability, I'm grateful for your powerful life force and strength. Knowing all this will pass, I love and cherish you even more, just as you are in this very moment.

LIVE BEAUTIFULLY, DIE BEAUTIFULLY— TODAY

Beginning Anew with a Sick or Dying Person

When someone we love is sick or dying, our natural impulse is to help—but often, we don't know how. In these moments, we can return to a simple practice called Beginning Anew. It helps us and our loved one release regrets, touch peace, and deepen connection.

This practice has four parts: Flower Watering, Expressing Regret, Expressing Hurt, and Making a Fresh Start. You do not always need to move through each step in order. Sometimes even a single sentence offered with true presence is enough.

1. Flower Watering

Begin by recognizing what is beautiful in the person's life. You might say, "Your life and your courage have inspired me," or simply, "Thank you for your love." Touch their hand, smile, and breathe quietly together. When someone is dying, hearing appreciation allows them to rest with peace.

2. Expressing Regret

If there is something you wish you had done differently, share this gently and without explanation: "I know I caused you pain, and I am sorry." There is no need to justify or reopen old wounds. Sincerity is enough. A simple acknowledgment can dissolve years of unspoken suffering.

3. Expressing Hurt

Sometimes we carry our own pain from the person who is ill or dying. Sharing it with mindfulness releases both sides. You might say, "When that happened, I felt hurt," or "There are things I still find difficult to understand." Speak from the heart, not the courtroom of the mind. As you speak, remember that this, too, is healing. If expressing hurt would cause harm or overwhelm, it may be wiser to hold it gently in your own heart. Stopping and deep looking enable our expressions to be skillful and beneficial for all involved.

4. Making a Fresh Start

Finally, invite a sense of renewal: "From today on, I wish to love you with more understanding," or "I'll do my best to continue you in myself as beautifully as possible." Even if the other person cannot respond, your intention plants a seed of reconciliation that continues in you both.

Each of these steps can be done silently, even from afar. What matters is the heart behind them—the wish for understanding, love, and forgiveness. Practicing Beginning Anew with someone who is dying helps both of you touch freedom. It reminds us that reconciliation does not end with death; it is a continuation of love itself.

Sariputra's Farewell

When Venerable Sariputra, one of the Buddha's closest disciples, felt that his time had come, he approached the Buddha and quietly asked for permission to enter Nirvana. The Buddha's response was simple and full of love and trust: "Do what you feel is timely." Sariputra then bowed and said, "If any word or deed of mine has ever caused you sorrow, please forgive me." The Buddha replied, "I forgive you, Sariputra. But there was not a single word or deed of yours that displeased me."[11]

This exchange reminds us of the tenderness possible at the end of life and the wish to leave nothing unresolved. To ask forgiveness and to offer it. To release one another with clarity and peace.

My grandmother, a simple woman without education, had the same kind of insight. She raised my brother and me with unwavering love and presence. Even when we had almost nothing, she was our stability—cooking for us, praying on her wooden plank bed, and offering a calmness that stayed with me long after I left Vietnam at seventeen. Her devotion was the first meditation practice I ever witnessed. In moments of difficulty, whether in America or later as a nun, the image of my grandmother sitting quietly with her rosary returned to me like a lantern in the dark.

Before she died, my grandmother told my aunt to bathe her and dress her in a special set of clothes. "I am going to a conference to meet the Buddha," grandmother said. "Don't cry for me or try to hold me back." She asked for the monk she had lovingly supported for many years to come and chant for her. Knowing Grandmother was near the end, Venerable Đồng Châu had come to stay on the third floor of our home. When he was told of her request, he immediately came downstairs. As he chanted, my grandmother brought her palms together to form a lotus bud, leaving just a little bit of space between her palms. My aunt instinctively reached out to help her hands meet, but Venerable Đồng Châu gently said, "Let Grandma be. She has already passed."

Grandmother died exactly as she had lived—clear, gentle, and fully at ease.

I did not learn of her passing until six months later. She had asked my relatives not to tell me and Sonny, fearing it would make us sad and disrupt our studies. When the news of her death finally reached me, it broke my heart. Yet later when I learned how my grandmother died, something inside me lightened. Her serenity lifted my grief and dispelled my fear of death. I realized dying beautifully is possible. Her death has been a profound gift of non-fear to those who remain.

Grandmother's way of dying has taught me how to live. Living beautifully is already dying beautifully. When we take care of our relationships, our thoughts, and our speech each day, we have nothing to hold back and nothing to regret.

Yet many of us spend our youth and good health focused on what we lack or resent, only to cling desperately to life when death approaches. As a doctor and a spiritual practitioner, I've come to see that those who fear death the most are often the ones who haven't truly lived.

One of my monastic sisters told me about her father's passing. He had copious diarrhea for days, even after he had stopped eating. She commented, "All our lives, we compete and cling to things—but on our deathbed, we can't even hold on to a single piece of shit!"

Her words may sound blunt, but they reveal a deep truth. The body eventually releases everything. Wealth, reputation, possessions, even dignity as we imagine it—all must be let go. Death humbles us completely. In the end, what truly matters is not what we have accumulated or defended, but the quality of our heart and the peace of our relationships.

Unresolved conflicts and unfinished business often drive our fear of death. Our desperation to live is not necessarily because our life is so meaningful that we want to live more. As a medical student and then a doctor, I sat with many dying patients, and many were severely depressed. Some kept looking out at the door, waiting for a loved one to come. In these cases, hardly anyone ever came—in life, the person hadn't taken care of their relationships. In pursuit of their career or other passions, they had severed or led superficial relationships with their spouses, partners, children, parents, and friends. So, in their dying hours, they waited for somebody to come to no avail.

I've also seen patients become so overwhelmed with anger that they screamed, hollered, and cursed at nurses and doctors.

Much of this suffering came from unfinished business—old wounds, regrets, and unspoken words that suddenly surfaced. Vietnamese tradition says that when we die, ghosts gather around us, taunting and frightening us. I believe these "ghosts" are often our own memories—the moments of our lives, the people we have loved and hurt, and those who have loved and hurt us. If we have not made peace with them, these memories can surge up from deep within our consciousness like a great wave in our dying hours.

This is why it's essential to care for our lives while we are still living—to tend to our relationships, bodies, thoughts, feelings, speech, and actions each day. This is the true coolness of Nirvana: a heart at peace, ready at any moment.

At the same time, not every death unfolds with such calm or clarity. Some people meet death in great pain, confusion, or fear. In those moments, we simply do the best we can—with the understanding, compassion, and presence available to us. Even a small moment of care, forgiveness, or mindful breathing can be enough.

Mending Broken Pieces with Gold

Even when life feels broken or tangled with regret or fear, it is never too late to begin again. As long as we are still breathing, something in our lives can still be repaired. A young person once said to me, "What is the point of believing in transformation? Next year will be just like last year!" When life feels repetitive and heavy with conflict, it can be hard to see why we should keep investing time, energy, and love in it.

When something precious is broken, we may think we have to throw it away even though it was once very precious to us. In the Japanese art of *kintsugi* ("golden joinery"), also known as *kintsukuroi* ("golden repair"), broken pottery is repaired by mending the areas of breakage with lacquer dusted or mixed with powdered gold. The vase is now whole, the cracks emphasized with gold. Rather than hiding the cracks, the repair highlights them. The vase or bowl, once repaired, becomes unique and beautiful.

The same can be true of our mistakes. We don't have to conceal them, reject them, or push them away. Instead, we can acknowledge them, breathe, soften, and express our regrets. This is the art of kintsugi—mending the broken pieces of our lives with honesty and dignity. When we reach the end of life, what matters most is not what we achieved, but what we have healed.

As long as we are alive, we have the opportunity to heal—both for ourselves and for those we love. In moments of deep despair, material wealth may hold little value, but mindful breathing can save our lives. Our spiritual practice can become the gold that mends the broken pieces of our lives and helps repair the connections between us. That is true gold. It reminds us to be in touch with our lives, still alive and still breathing, no matter how difficult the situation may be or how close to death we are.

It is possible to support someone's peaceful and meaningful death. The practice of Beginning Anew shared previously can help a dying person make peace with their life and their approaching death. I have sat with people in this practice, helping them reconcile with themselves and their loved ones.

In those moments, they express deep appreciation for their spouses and children—and in return, their loved ones share heartfelt gratitude with them as they lie on their deathbed.

Often, tears flow, words long unspoken are finally offered, and something softens in the room. What once felt broken begins to mend. Like the vase repaired with gold, the cracks are still visible, but they no longer need to be hidden. Sometimes the most beautiful moments of a life appear in its final hours. When reconciliation becomes possible—even at the end—a person can leave this world with a lighter heart, and those who remain carry less sorrow forward.

I share these stories not as a standard anyone must meet, but simply as an inspiration. Every life and every death unfolds under different conditions, and we do the best we can with the time and awareness we have.

LIVE BEAUTIFULLY, DIE BEAUTIFULLY— TODAY

Sending Energy to a Sick or Dying Person

When someone we love is suffering or nearing death, we may feel powerless. Yet in truth, we always have something to offer: our steadiness, our breath, our love. Energy is not limited by time, distance, or circumstance. When we are calm and clear, our presence itself becomes a source of support.

You can send healing and supportive energy to a friend or loved one who is sick, dying, or has recently passed away. This can be done individually, as a family, or as a community. This practice helps acknowledge the reality of the situation and serves as an expression of love, care, and presence. It can offer immense comfort and strength.

Begin by sitting quietly. Rest your body. Let your breathing become natural. Once you feel settled enough, bring the image of the person to mind as you breathe in. As you breathe out, send them peace. You might silently say:

Breathing in, I send you my peace.
Breathing out, I send you my love.

If you like, place a hand over your heart or gently in front of you and see if you can feel warmth moving outward. There is no need to push or visualize forcefully—only to rest in connection. The quality of your presence is the true offering.

If the person is nearby, you may hold their hand, or simply sit together in silence. If they are far away, trust the field of interbeing that connects you. Whether they are aware or not, your calm presence contributes to their ease.

After a few minutes, you can dedicate the energy you have generated:

May this peace reach you.
May you be free from pain and from fear.
May you touch the joy and spaciousness of the present moment.

When we practice like this, we touch the truth that love is not bound by the body. Even when someone passes away, our love continues as a current of healing energy in the world.

4

All that is
dear to me
and everyone
I love are of the
nature to change.
There is no
way to escape
being separated
from them.

The people, places, and stories we treasure are not ours to keep, but ours to accompany for a time. Sooner or later, everything we love will change. To be alive is to be in constant relation with change—and to be shaped by it. This remembrance does not come to rob us of our joy, but to deepen it. It introduces a kind of sacred sorrow: an understanding that nothing lasts, and because nothing lasts, everything matters. Grief, in this way, is not a failure of love but its continuation. To love without clinging is one of the fiercest and most freeing practices we can undertake. As we loosen our grip, we find that affection does not need possession to be real. What it asks of us is simpler and harder: to be present while we can, to care while we can, and to cherish each moment while it is here.

Thầy's Stroke in 2014

One of the most painful aspects of impermanence can be watching the people we love change before our eyes. Illness, aging, and loss remind us that even our greatest teachers and companions cannot remain with us in the same form forever.

I was at Magnolia Grove Monastery when Thầy suffered a major stroke in October 2014. As one of the elder nuns, I felt it was essential to remain steady and calm for the entire Sangha. We immediately held a Beginning Anew Ceremony to pray for Thầy.

The next day, we held a Tea-in, gathering to drink tea and share stories about our love for Thầy and the impact he had on our lives. Many beautiful reflections were offered—some joyful, others emotional and deeply moving. Coming together helped us support one another through the shock of Thầy's stroke and was a truly meaningful way to hold space for our emotions, embracing them as a community.

Night after night, I would go to the meditation hall, put on my *sanghati*—the outer monastic robe worn during formal practice—and chant Thầy's translation of the Heart Sutra, *The Insight that Brings Us to the Other Shore*. In our tradition, chanting is not only recitation but a way of breathing and concentrating to embody the Dharma. As I chanted, I called upon the insight of the Buddha and Thầy to support me through that difficult time.

The most recent translation of the Heart Sutra had just been completed by Thầy in August 2014, and Brother Pháp Linh had composed music for it. It was the most beautiful—and also the most challenging—chant I had ever practiced. I listened to the recorded version through headphones and chanted along, gradually learning the chant by heart. Later, Sister Bội Nghiêm and I began leading sessions to teach the Sangha how to chant it. Chanting helped us release our emotions, open our hearts, and connect with Thầy's spiritual energy. Gradually, we grew more confident in chanting *The Insight that Brings Us to the Other Shore*. From that time on, I have always chanted this sutra from the depths of my heart.[12]

In the years that followed, Thầy continued to live among us in a quiet, transformed way. Though his words were no longer able to teach as before, his presence had always been the true teacher and remained a steady source of inspiration for the Sangha. We cared for him with tenderness, and he continued to guide us—sometimes with a small gesture, sometimes simply through his being.

In January 2022, Thầy released his body. By then, he had prepared us for many years to see his continuation beyond form.

A Cloud Never Dies

I wrote the following letter to Thầy two years after he passed. Writing it helped me touch his presence and continue my relationship with him, even as the form I loved had changed.

Dear Thầy,

You have become a cloud for over two years now. For so long, you prepared us for the day you would leave your physical form. I recall one of your early Dharma talks, in my first year as a novice. You held up your passport and said calmly, "Thầy just renewed his passport recently, and Thầy is aware that it may be Thầy's last passport." Those words struck me like thunder. For years afterward, I carried that image in my meditation on impermanence. I learned not to look for you only in your familiar, endearing form, but to touch you in my breath, in my steps, and in asking myself, "Would Thầy think this? Would Thầy speak this way? Would Thầy act like this?"

News of your passing arrived during a ceremony for Sister Chỉ Nghiêm, who had recently passed away. One sister gasped, and the hall fell into a long, deep silence. I stayed with my breathing, steadying myself with a deep conviction, "Thầy, you are here. You are in me." When we stepped out of the meditation hall, an elder brother asked me to say a few words before our walking meditation to the Ksitigarbha Grove to spread Sister Chỉ Nghiêm's ashes. I shared that our loved ones continue in us when we live fully and beautifully.

Your body was gone, but your essence had already been transmitted into each of us. We could touch you in every mindful breath and step.

Later that afternoon, I brought several young sisters to your hut, where I had kept your framed photograph, the altar table, and all the small objects needed for your memorial—down to the white sand for the incense urn. Everything had been carefully prepared. Two young brothers arrived with a truck, and within an hour, your altar was established in the Ocean of Peace Meditation Hall. The schedule for the seven-day "Heart Recollection Retreat—Coming and Going In Freedom," also already prepared, began immediately.

And yet, no amount of planning could soften the ache of losing the teacher we love. What helped more than anything was the Noble Silence of those seven days. That shared silence held us like a bowl. Lay friends joined us—some for the full retreat, others for a single day—and they too entered the silence. There was no need for condolences. We moved like bees in a beehive: steady, connected, and spacious enough for anyone who wished to enter. As a community, we honored you by practicing exactly what you had taught us—walking meditatively, eating in silence, reciting the Mindfulness Trainings together. You were not gone. You were everywhere.

Among all the moments of that week, one experience revealed to me most clearly the power of the practice. On the fifth day of the Heart Recollection Retreat, I had a dream about you. I entered a small, cozy room and found you sitting there alone, peaceful. I sat quietly on the floor. No words passed between us. Suddenly, in the dream, I understood: Thầy had passed away. Yet there was no shock, no sorrow—only calm, deep peace. My mind, trained by years of practice, could receive loss without collapsing beneath it in a way that had been unimaginable to me when loved ones had died in the past.

For more than twenty years after my mother died, she would be unable to see or speak to me when she appeared in my dreams. Each time I dreamed of her, I awoke feeling abandoned. After John died and I became a nun, it took a year for my mind to accept his absence in a dream in which I looked frantically for him until I suddenly realized he couldn't attend my birthday because he had died—not because he had forgotten or he had abandoned me.

But with you, dear Thầy, it took only five days for my store consciousness to acknowledge your passing. Five days for the deepest layers of my mind to say "yes" to what had happened. That is the fruit of the practice, and it has helped me touch peace in my grief—for you and for John. I am healing. My heart is becoming steadier, clearer, more spacious.

What has been given remains. Your transmission continues. You are alive in my every day and every mindful breath, beloved Thầy.

Your child, Dang Nghiem

Thầy's Relics

The summer after Thầy's passing, I went to Plum Village for the ceremonial spreading of Thầy's ashes. New Hamlet hosted over eight hundred retreatants from all hamlets attending the Summer Retreat in a solemn, reverent ceremony. Afterward, some of Thầy's ashes remained! I respectfully asked for a small, rounded relic and placed it carefully in a container. Later that day, when I opened the lid, I discovered it was no longer solid; it had turned to dust.

Back at Deer Park, I kept Thầy's relic above my bed for several months. One day, reflecting once more on what to do with it, I decided to place it in my cup, add water, and join my palms in reverence as I drank it. With each sip and mindful breath, I felt Thầy's relic become a part of me. From time to time, I reflect on that special moment of union with Thầy's very flesh.

The actions I took after Thầy's death and the message of this dream both grow from the connection we cultivated while he was alive. My experience is a reminder and a mindfulness bell: When you are with someone, be present for them. Put aside your phone and look into their eyes. Ask questions out of curiosity and care. It is not the virtual, abstract world that drives connection, but cherishing what is alive and here in front of us before it is too late. Do not allow yourself to become distant from those around you. When change inevitably comes, we are broken and our lives are shattered if we are not present to reality.

Looking Directly at Change

Many people ask whether it's morbid to contemplate the Five Remembrances. A young practitioner once told me she practiced with them simply because she was advised to. Then, one day in the shower, a clump of hair came off in her hands. She panicked—until the thought arose, "I am of the nature to grow old. I am of the nature to have ill-health." Instantly, she calmed down. Practice had become her refuge, ready when need arose.

Suffering does not come from being subject to birth, growth, change, and death. Fear, denial, and refusal to look at these truths and how they shape our thoughts, speech, and behaviors is what makes us suffer. When we practice inhabiting the body with awareness and embracing its changes, we train ourselves not to be shocked by them. We soften the tension that comes from pretending we will not age or fall ill and make a life with less suffering possible, regardless of what happens.

Breathing in, I recognize the lines on my forehead, the soreness in my knees.

Breathing out, I thank my body for doing its best.

Our culture often reinforces denial through cosmetic interventions and a hunger for digital immortality. Even medical professionals sometimes cling to normalcy, pretending nothing is wrong after a serious diagnosis until the realities of illness are forced upon us. I knew someone whose mother worked throughout her final weeks with cancer. Since she acted as though nothing was wrong, that was what her children believed. When she "suddenly" died, they felt betrayed and unprepared—not because she had died, but because they had been kept in the dark about the imminence of her death.

To come back to the breath is to come back to life.

"Hello, my in-breath. Hello, my out-breath. Thank you for this life."

In Spanish, there is a phrase *¡Qué lástima!*—what could have been. Dreams and memories are beautiful, but they are not a home. Only the present moment is real.

Desire pulls our minds into the past and future:

"I wish that had happened."

"I hope that will happen."

When I was twelve, my mother went to the market and never returned. Decades later, I am now older than my mother ever was. For years, I wondered what might have been different if she had lived. On his first trip back to Vietnam, my brother whispered to me on the plane, "What if mother is still alive and comes to find us?" Sonny was twenty-two by then, and I was twenty-six; his words revealed how tenderly the past can cling to us.

Yet I have learned that my mother has not truly left me, even though we were separated in form. You may never have met my mother, but when you look at me, you are seeing her. The Fourth Remembrance teaches that we will inevitably be separated from the people we love, yet separation does not mean the end of love. To live deeply in the present does not mean forgetting—it means allowing our love for those who change form to continue expressing itself in the way we live, breathe, and care for others. Love always unfolds now.

The practice of loving-kindness teaches us to begin in the love within and expand outward. This universal prayer, common to all Buddhist traditions in some form, can be expressed like this:

> *May I be happy. May I be safe. May all beings live in peace and security—near or far, visible or invisible, born or yet to be born.*

When we see the suffering of the world—war, hunger, loss—we may feel insignificant. Yet each of us makes up someone's world. Every action, every word, every breath matters.

The Paradoxes of Grief

Grief is full of contradictions and paradoxes. When someone we love changes form or is no longer physically present, grief naturally appears. It is one of the ways love continues to express itself.

From what I have known of grief, this is what I know to be true: You may feel utterly lost, confused, and out of sync with everything in your life, yet you're expected to keep up with daily routines and a semblance of normalcy. You have to eat, drink, use the bathroom, maintain your appearance. You may want nothing more than to collapse, shut down, or even disappear, yet you're expected to smile, to speak, and even to console others as they grieve, too.

The business of living becomes a burden, yet others count on your presence and comfort. They reach for your attention, but are met with hollow eyes and limp arms and feel betrayed.

Your goals and ambitions may feel meaningless now, and yet, responsibilities persist. Work continues. Life continues. And you wonder: Why keep living when everything feels heavy and hollow?

Your thoughts turn longingly toward the one you've lost. Your heart breaks in their absence. Alongside the love, there may be anger, resentment, frustration, or even a sense of betrayal for being left to face this chaos alone.

Grief also reveals who your real friends are, and who offers only empty words or none at all. You're surrounded by people, yet you may feel completely isolated. How is it possible that someone doesn't even know the name of your beloved? The future seems blank, unknowable, yet you may be told to "be strong," to "hold it together," to "move on."

With death, everything shared in the past feels gone, your imagined future wiped out. And yet, memories are the only things that feel real now. You're haunted by regrets, by what could have been, by what should have been, by relentless what-ifs. Every cell aches, and you feel numb to the core. All you want is to crawl into bed and weep endlessly, drawing the curtains tight, shutting every door, letting the world darken to match your insides. Even then, the loneliness is so vast that you long to disappear into a crowd, to feel anything other than aloneness.

You move through life like the walking dead, yet your luminous grief draws others in. You want to collapse into someone's arms, to be held and forgotten, but the fear of more betrayal, more loss keeps you distant.

It feels like the end of everything. And yet, a faint, persistent hope for real peace remains. However small, however quiet, it is your guiding light.

LIVE BEAUTIFULLY, DIE BEAUTIFULLY— TODAY

Being Your Own Safe Harbor

In this practice, we come home to the one place that has never left us: our own breath, our own body, our own presence. To take refuge in ourselves is to rediscover a quiet trust that has been here all along—a trust that can hold us through fear, change, and uncertainty. Living beautifully and dying beautifully begins with learning to be a safe place for ourselves. With each breath, we can return, soften, and feel the ground beneath our own feet.

Find a posture—seated, standing, or lying down—that feels natural and supportive and where you can remain alert. Let your body settle, soften your shoulders, and come home to your breath. There is nowhere to rush, nothing to force. Simply arrive.

Breathing in, I arrive in my body.
Breathing out, I relax.

Breathing in, I feel my body sitting here.
Breathing out, I allow my body to soften.

Breathing in, I entrust myself to my body.
Breathing out, I am grateful to my body for taking care of me day after day.

Breathing in, I recognize that my body entrusts itself to me.
Breathing out, I vow to be kinder and more attentive in caring for my body.

Breathing in, I entrust myself to me.
Breathing out, I vow to be kinder and more attentive in caring for myself.

Breathing in, I am safe.

Breathing out, I am at home.

Remain with your breathing for a few more moments. Feel the quiet presence of your body supporting you, the steady rhythm of your breath continuing without effort.

As you rest here, notice that safe harbor is not something you have to build or earn. It is here whenever you return with awareness and kindness. From this place of steadiness, we can meet life's joys and losses with tenderness. When we know how to be a refuge for ourselves, we can also become a refuge for others.

Living beautifully and dying beautifully begin in these small moments of returning—one breath, one step, one act of care at a time.

When Love Is the Practice

For as long as I can remember, fear has been part of my love for my brother. Long before politics entered our relationship, I feared I might lose Sonny suddenly, without warning. Sometimes separation happens through death, but sometimes it begins long before—when a person's views, identity, or way of seeing the world changes so much that we no longer recognize the person we thought we knew.

During one memorable presidential election, I discovered my brother fully supported a candidate whose positions seemed inhuman to me. One day, he said, "All the immigrants will take away jobs." I stared at him in shock, my mouth hanging open.

"What do you mean?" I asked, stunned. I had no idea he held those views—we had never talked about politics with each other before. I told him, "Sonny, stop. Stop, honey. Aren't we immigrants? Aren't we refugees?"

My brother's extreme views have only grown more entrenched over time. Sonny became completely anti-immigrant, anti-prisoner—anti-everything. During one heated exchange, he said, "You're one of those elites—so educated and liberal—that you've lost touch with reality." I just sat there, thinking, "He's against everything . . . and I'm the one out of touch!"

When it comes to politics, my brother is what I call a "big splasher." He throws everything at you, more than willing to drown you. He doesn't want to discuss—he wants to fight. I've learned not to engage in politics with my brother. When someone is a big splasher, don't splash back. Don't fight. I had to remember I can only take care of my own thoughts, words, and actions. His views, his choices, and his path are not mine to control.

Sometimes, this practice unfolds in very ordinary moments. Recently, my brother drove me back to the monastery from my niece's school—a thirty-minute drive. He talked nonstop about politics. I tried to steer the conversation elsewhere, but it was futile.

Near the monastery, Sonny turned to his daughter, who was thirteen and looked incredibly bored, and said, "Maybe I should speak in another language so it doesn't affect Sunee so much." I replied, "Yes, if you spoke French, it would be much more palatable for me." We laughed. Humor helped.

When we understand interbeing, we choose family. We choose love and harmony. If we cling tightly to views, we lose each other. I've told my brother many times, "Politicians come and go, but we are blood for life." As we neared the monastery, almost as if to spite me, Sonny added, "Remember when I called you to bail me out of jail while you were in college? I actually had the money. I just wanted yours to spend. And those times I said I was suicidal? I just needed your sympathy and some cash." He paused. "Do you hate me? Would you have helped me if you knew the truth?"

I sat in silence, stunned. Deep down, I knew my brother had been sincere when he'd reached out during those dark moments. So, I looked at him and said, "Honey, if it was to save your life, I would do anything for you. And yes—I would do it all over again."

When I stepped out of the car that day, Sonny hugged me. Then he pulled out his wallet and took out $200. For years, I hadn't accepted his money—he works too hard for it, fixing cars in the scorching Arizona heat.

I turned to my niece and said, "Your dad is bribing me because he just traumatized me. So, I'll accept his money." We laughed again. More importantly, my brother drove away without anger, and I walked away still having my brother. Even when Sonny tries to provoke me, I laugh. Underneath every argument, every moment of tension, I see the same thing again and again: my fear of losing my brother. When I worry about his diabetes and health in general, and he doesn't listen, I text him and say: "I love you, my dear. I just want you to be safe and happy. I want you to be there for your daughter."

The day after our drive was Sonny's birthday. As much as I dreaded seeing him, I still showed up. We had a wonderful time playing volleyball with Sunee and later shared a meal with his landlord and their relatives. At the end of the evening, Sonny walked me to my car. We embraced tightly. Then he looked at me and said, "Please forgive my sins." His voice was tender, sincere. I replied, "And please forgive my sins."

If something had happened to me after that moment—if it was the last time I ever saw my brother—I would be at peace.

I only have one brother. Even when our mother was still alive, I took care of him. After she disappeared, I continued to raise him. Now he's fifty-three years old, but when I think of him, tears still come. That fear of losing my brother—it's always been there. I practice with it, because fear that we don't take care of or understand keeps us from living fully. So, I sit with it. I breathe with it.

When my niece came along, my fear of loss expanded to include her. Loving deeply means risking grief. As a nun, I rarely leave the monastery unless it's truly necessary. Still, I make every effort to be present for my niece. My presence is the greatest gift I can offer her. When impermanence and change touch us, I will not regret that I wasn't there.

When we love someone, fear of loss naturally arises. If we're not mindful, that fear can consume us, and then we miss the person who is still right in front of us. We fail to cherish them. We lose each other long before death arrives—through stubborn views, wounded pride, or the refusal to listen. Through awareness, we heal. We transform fear into love. We take care of our relationships, here and now. One day Sonny and I will be separated—all of us will be separated. This is the truth of the Fourth Remembrance. Knowing this helps me remember what truly matters: not winning arguments, not defending my views, but loving while we are still here, even as we change.

Embrace Fear and Protect the Mind of Love

This teaching also applies to the fear we may feel toward people who look different from us or who believe differently. We build walls out of fear, and those walls prevent us from connecting, from seeing clearly, from loving fully. So let us breathe with our fears. Smile at them. Above all—let us choose love. Let us choose harmony and peace, again and again, even when it's not easy. This is what protects us and the world around us.

Though we pride ourselves on being highly developed, we should also be aware that our animal ancestors are alive and well in us. Deep in the brain, the systems that protect life can still take the lead—when the emotional brain is triggered, strong reactions arise and survival reflexes take over. In those moments, we may react before understanding what is really happening.

The views and stories we consume unmindfully through news, social media, and the people around us can quietly plant seeds of fear and distrust. Without awareness of our body, thoughts, and speech, these seeds may go unnoticed as they sprout and encourage us to treat people differently and look at them with suspicion or even paranoia. Over time, subtle biases can harden into righteousness that leads us to defend positions and actions we never consciously chose. Mindfulness lets us notice the body's alarms, breathe, and choose again so safety can begin within and spread outward.

Breathe into whatever fear may be present. Smile.

Relax your whole body. Let love and peace fill this very moment.

We may make many sacrifices for those we love while neglecting our own safety and peace. When we choose hatred, enmity, or discrimination and cause harm to others through our thoughts, speech, or behaviors, we harm ourselves first and foremost. The truth is the mind of love itself is our only child. It is what we must care for and protect most dearly.

When we lose trust in love, we suffer deeply. Many people search for love through romantic or sexual relationships, hoping to feel a sense of connection and belonging but finding disappointment and despair. Sometimes, they lose faith in love altogether and start to believe that love is only a game. When that belief takes root, they may become bitter and destructive toward themselves and others.

But as a mother risks her life for her child, we must also be willing to risk everything to protect our mind of love, for our own peace, safety, and healing—and for the peace, safety, and healing of others. This means choosing love, peace, and harmony over our personal views and ideas, again and again. Protecting the mind of love helps us remember what truly matters: connection, understanding, and care. From this ground, our actions become clearer and more courageous. Justice and protection of life can only grow from a mind that is not ruled by fear or hatred. When love is protected within us, our actions in the world naturally protect life as well. This is what we learn to do in our families, our communities, and in the wider world—we are all brothers and sisters. We come back to love. Again and again.

I Love You, Trump

Recently, I went on a teaching tour for Vietnamese youth, known as Viet Wake Up. When I boarded the plane, all the aisle and window seats were already taken—only middle seats remained. I noticed a middle seat in the first row that had extra legroom because it was by the door and the wing, and I headed toward it.

As I approached, the woman in the aisle seat looked me up and down from head to toe with clear disgust. From that one glance, a feeling of coldness and hostility unfolded. Though I thought, "I probably shouldn't sit here; she clearly doesn't like me," I knew I'd end up in a middle seat somewhere. At least this one had extra space. So, I asked, as softly as I could, "May I please sit here?"

She didn't respond, but just looked down. I took a breath and swallowed my pride, quietly, sitting down next to her. After settling in, I turned to her and said, "That's such a beautiful color you have on." She was wearing an elegant, striking, fuchsia vest that really suited her. When I complimented her, she looked genuinely surprised. After a moment, she replied, "Oh. I like it too."

And just like that, something shifted. Bit by bit, we started talking. Before I knew it, she was telling me about her life—how she had been abandoned as a child, raised in a foster home, and suffered abuse. Then she began to cry. Moved by her vulnerability, I gently placed my hand on her face.

Just minutes earlier, we had been tense, distant, even adversarial strangers. Now, as she opened her heart to me, I could sit beside her and offer comfort wrapped in deep, human connection.

As we continued talking, I shared that my brother holds political views very different from my own. She looked at me, a little sheepish, and said, "I'm very conservative." Of course, I already knew that. Yet the way she said it—so soft, so gentle—touched me. I placed my hand on her chest and said, "But your heart is wide open."

Seeing more than this person's negative reaction toward me, I was able to connect with her. I saw she was wearing a beautiful color. I saw she was suffering. I saw her pain. We were able to connect not because we agreed on everything, but because we were willing to see each other beyond our views.

Whether we support or oppose a particular leader or ideology is not really the point. Each of us carries within ourselves many different views, fears, and hopes. At times, we may be open and compassionate. At other times we may become fearful, defensive, or biased. These are not labels that belong to one group—they are human tendencies that exist in all of us.

Some leaders are very skilled at watering seeds of division and hatred. Unfortunately, many of us get pulled into that and allow fear, suspicion, uncertainty, even deep hatred to grow. When we face people who seem to have lost touch with their own humanity and who disregard the well-being of others, we must protect our own humanity first. We must protect our own goodness. If we lose that, we only add to the despair and suffering in the world.

One day, while sitting in meditation, a thought arose in me: "I love you, Trump." It startled me. "Did I just think that?" Then it came again: "I love you." And it kept coming, throughout that day, and in the days that followed. Now, I can say it naturally: "I love you, Trump."

True awakening is always possible. We can always use our power to heal instead of divide. Awakening ripples out and transforms countless lives. Even if awakening in the other person never happens, the thought that it could helps lighten my own heart. It helps preserve my mind of love, my compassion, and my faith in humanity.

The practice is very simple, though not always easy. We return to our breath. We may say quietly to ourselves, "May my heart remain open, even to people like you." Or simply, "You are not outside of me." If it helps, you might practice with a name that challenges you—someone close to you, or even a public figure you struggle to understand. Offer them love, understanding, and compassion. Not necessarily because they will change, and not because we agree with them, but because protecting the mind of love is the only way we can remain fully human. When we allow hatred to take root in us, we lose something precious in ourselves. And if we lose our capacity to love, we have already lost far more than any political argument.

What's Right and What's Wrong?

One night, I couldn't sleep for three or four hours. When I finally fell asleep, I dreamed I was talking with a monk when I suddenly stood up, made a hand-waving gesture, and simply walked away. As I moved off, I stopped just within his line of sight and thought to myself, "What has become of us? We used to count on each other, and now I just walk away." I felt a deep sadness. Even in the dream, I recognized that my action was unskillful.

Something similar had happened in real life, but reversed. I had been speaking with a monastic brother, sharing something very personal, when he abruptly said, "I need to go get some food," and walked away. I was left unsure—did he not realize the depth of what I was sharing? Did he disagree with me? Or was he simply too hungry to stay present? In waking life, I had been left behind. Being the one walking away in my dream made me pause and reconsider my own actions.

In a world filled with hatred, discrimination, violence, and confusion, we often ask ourselves, "How do I know what's right? How do I know what's wrong?" The insight of interbeing—the understanding that everything is interconnected—is a mirror for our thoughts, speech, and behavior that helps us to find our way. When someone hurts me, instead of getting caught in repetitive thoughts about the harm they've caused, I can try to see myself in their situation. I, too, have hurt others—sometimes unknowingly, sometimes knowingly. What kind of pain was I in when I acted in hurtful ways? How was I also, deep down, hurt when I caused harm? As a result, I've come to understand my own mind more and to see that I usually hurt others when I am suffering myself—when I am in pain, emotionally or physically. As the saying goes, "Hurt people hurt people."

When we see our own suffering clearly, the line between what is "right" and "wrong" becomes less rigid and more compassionate. We begin to understand how easily people hurt each other when they are in pain. When we remember we will be separated from all we love, we become more careful with our words, our gestures, and even the moments when we turn away from one another. A conversation left unfinished, a person walking away, a heart that closes are small moments that can become the quiet beginnings of separation. Remembering impermanence helps us pause, breathe, and turn back toward one another while we still can.

Dealing with Difficult Relationships

Practicing the Five Remembrances can help us cultivate acceptance—of ourselves, our lives, those we love, and even those with whom we experience difficulties and conflict. All that is dear to me, and everyone I love, are of a nature to change. Not only are we of the nature to change, but everyone we love or hate is of the nature to change. There's no way to escape impermanence.

We suffer because we have to be separated from those we love. We also suffer because we have to be close to those we dislike or hate. Oblivious to impermanence, we often don't pay attention to those who we love, who are nearest to us, as we should. We think, "Oh, they will always be there." Yet that is not true. It has never been true.

There's a story about a master and his disciple. The disciple often asked to go on a picnic, but the teacher was always too busy. Each time, he'd say, "A picnic sounds like a wonderful idea—we'll do it one of these days." But that day kept getting postponed, stretching from one year to the next.

One day, as they were traveling together, their path was blocked by a funeral procession. The teacher asked, "What's happening over there?"

The disciple replied, "They're going on a picnic."

We often assume there will be more time—tomorrow, next year—to be with our loved ones. When change strikes, we're left not only with the pain of loss, but also with the weight of regret and unresolved emotions.

Speaking from personal experience, I truly believed John would be there with me in old age. Then one day, he was gone—and I was only thirty-one. The pain of guilt, regret, and resentment can cut deeper than the grief itself. It's the pain of having taken someone for granted, of not being there and understanding their pain or seeing that they were always changing and, like all things, would not be with us forever.

If we acknowledge this in our daily life, we will express acknowledgment, appreciation, and support more often and more generously. "I know you are there, and I'm so happy. Thank you for being my partner, for being my child, for being my mother, my father." Just this simple practice can change everything in a relationship. We can acknowledge, "You're not perfect. You cause me pain, but I am also thankful you are a part of my life. Thank you."

When we don't get along so well with someone, we may secretly or openly wish to get rid of them. Yet when they are far away, we may be just as miserable! Even if someone new comes along, they may remind you of that unpleasant person from your past. I have heard this often from visitors to Deer Park. Even after a divorce, you marry someone new—fresh and wonderful at first—but over time find yourself wondering, "Did I just marry the same unpleasant person all over again?" Déjà vu is a reminder that we ourselves haven't really changed. An eraser with a stain will smear a brand-new board. Instead of trying to get rid of somebody because you don't have a good relationship, see if you can change your way of thinking, speaking, and behaving. Ultimately, whatever arises from our mind creates our reality.

The mind of discrimination, hatred, resentment, and pain from our past colors our views. It is a lens through which we look at others. We are the ones who see people and situations, familiar and new, through the same tinted lens. Mindfulness practice helps us remove those filters and allows us to begin anew, with ourselves and with others.

My Mother and Me

I had a turbulent relationship with my mother, despite the fact that she disappeared when I was only twelve. Raised largely by my grandmother, I lived with my mother for less than six years in total, and even during that time, she was often away working. In total, I probably spent only a few months with her. Still, in that short time, my mother left a lasting impact. Her verbal and physical abuse caused me a great deal of pain.

My mother had been cruel to me at times. After she disappeared, I believed she was a witch who'd gone straight to hell. With time, I realized how harsh my mother's life had been. Imagine a young teenage girl leaving the countryside for the city to earn money to support her family. She became a maid, ran away from the abusive circumstances that developed in that job, and then ended up with American GIs before giving birth to my brother and me. What other options did an uneducated country girl have? What other options do the poor young women in war-torn countries have? All alone in the city, my mother had to hustle to survive and to provide for her family back in the countryside. The hard life hardened her heart toward even her own daughter. As I grew older and matured in my spiritual practice, I came to understand how much my mother suffered in her thirty-six years. My mother never had a chance to sit peacefully, to walk leisurely, to be at ease in her body. She was always working, always struggling to make ends meet, and she became angry, bitter, and abusive.

My mother had done her best, and now I thank her for what she *was* able to do: "Thank you, mother, for working so hard and providing for your family." I was never left hungry. When I look at childhood photographs, I recognize that I was always nicely dressed. Even though my mother wasn't around much, I was well cared for because she chose to bring my grandmother to live with us.

I certainly appreciate the good things that happened to me, but I have also learned to be thankful for the things that didn't happen to me, that weren't given to me, and even the things that were taken away from me. For example, a deep gratitude came to me in walking meditation one day, "Thank you, Mother, for not aborting me!" As we mend the cracks in our spirit with the *kintsugi* gold of our mindfulness practice, we can even learn to be thankful for our pain; without it, transformation and renewal would not be possible.

We all have seeds of bias toward ourselves and others. Mindfulness helps us recognize and transform these seeds before they manifest as harm. When we sit quietly and check in with our body and breath, we can stop running from pain and truly face life. We can look at the broken pieces of our lives and use the gold of mindful breathing, mindful walking, loving speech and deep listening to seal the broken pieces and to heal our relationships.

I say to my mother in me, "Mother, I'm healing for you. I'm living a life of freedom for you." Learning to sit for my mother, to walk for my mother, and to heal for my mother has made our relationship so much more peaceful and healthier than it was forty some years ago. It is through practice that we learn to make peace with our loved ones while they are still alive and even after they have passed away. Whatever they were unable to do in their lifetimes, we can carry forward and fulfill for them.

Not long ago, I dreamed my mother was lying on her side, and I was lying behind her on mine. My brother was behind me, also lying on his side. We didn't say anything, but it was a tender, peaceful moment of gently cradling one another.

The Importance of Grief

Thầy shared that when somebody we love changes or passes away, a part of us dies with that person. At the same time, because we are still alive, our beloved has a chance to live on. Rumi is said to have written, "When we are dead, seek not our tomb in the earth, but find it in the hearts of men."[13] When separation comes, grief arises naturally. Grief is not a failure of practice. It is the heart's response to love meeting impermanence.

My mother passed away forty-five years ago, and my partner more than twenty-five years ago, yet they are still alive within me. I see my mother in my bright smile. Her grace and eloquence are part of me, and so too is her capacity for anger and sharp speech. I see John in the purple flowers along the sidewalk, in nature, in the sunrise and the sunset, in the coconut lotion that I still use until this day. I've learned to nurture the beautiful and endearing aspects of my loved ones so they can continue to bloom within me and even *become* me. My grandmother was spiritual and wise, and it's because of her that I walk this path today.

When we speak of grief, we often think of losing one person we love. Yet separation from what we love does not only occur through death. Sometimes it happens through war, migration, or history itself. Entire communities carry grief born from war, displacement, exile, and the loss of belonging. These wounds can last for generations, shaping families and cultures long after the original events have passed. For many people, grief is not only about the loss of someone dear, but also the loss of a homeland, a language, or a way of life that can never fully be recovered.

Yet when a loved one does die, we are confronted with the raw truth of separation. The form we knew is no longer there in the same way. I once saw an art piece that stayed with me. The artist had shaped wire into the form of a woman curled in the fetal position. Inside her, heavy stones filled the empty space. The piece was titled "The Weight of Grief." I knew exactly what that meant. I've felt that weight myself—first with the passing of my grandmother, and later with the death of my partner. There's no way to avoid pain and grief. No spiritual practice, no amount of mindful breathing or deep relaxation can take it away entirely. The pain remains.

While we cannot escape pain, we can learn to hold it rather than letting it consume or destroy us. When we stay with grief long enough, insight can appear. The Buddha often taught that reality is not as simple as "gone" or "still here."

That is why it is essential to live deeply after loss. In doing so, we allow our loved ones to continue living—within us, through us, in the rhythm of our daily lives. They are not only present in our hearts, but also in our families, relatives, children, and grandchildren.

In the Buddhist tradition, this is sometimes understood through the insight of "neither the same nor different." The one who continues is not exactly the same person in the same form, and yet not entirely different either. Imagine a candle burning steadily, radiating light and warmth. You can use that flame to light another candle. Have you ever wondered if the flame on the second candle is the same as the first or different? In truth, it is neither the same nor entirely different. Reality isn't always so neatly divided—it flows continuously, but our minds and cultures often try to fit things into tidy categories.

Now imagine the first flame is blown out. The second candle still burns with the flame that came from the first. Is the original flame gone? Or does it live on? This question becomes very real when we face loss. When we love someone deeply, they become part of who we are. That's why losing them feels like losing a piece of ourselves. But because they become part of us, they are not truly gone. Their light still burns within us.

Whenever I visit my niece, Sunee, I experience this clearly. The moment she opens the door, I'm transported. Her face, so much like my mother's, brings my mother back to me. In

Sunee, I see my mother's spirit, transformed: radiant, youthful, healthy, eyes full of light, and a smile that could brighten any room. In moments like these, separation feels less final. This does not erase the pain, but it helps us understand it differently.

How we move through loss is not just a personal journey. When trauma strikes, it brings deep pain within ourselves, our families, and our communities. We need time and space our society rarely allows to acknowledge that pain and the weight of grief. We can create an altar with a photo of our loved one and place fresh flowers there each day. On special occasions like anniversaries or birthdays, we can prepare their favorite dish. These acts are ways of honoring their memory and saying, "You were part of my life, and you're still here in my heart. You're not gone, finished, or forgotten. You're woven into the very fabric of my being."

Rushing forward can be a way of running from grief. But grief is not a detour; it is a path forward that shapes whether we heal or remain wounded, whether we move toward liberation or stay entangled in unprocessed and unresolved pain. When grieving is denied, so is healing. So is transformation. We block the understanding that can only come from sitting with our sorrow. Grieving is not optional; it is essential. When we allow grief to breathe, it sometimes speaks through us. During one such moment, these words came to me:

All that Remains

Thank you, my dear, for crying this morning.
Your choked sobs gave my heart permission
to burst through walls of self-defense.
So that I, too, may cry—
For the person who just passed away,

her memorial photo still fragrant with the scent of fresh ink—
also for those who have passed through my life.
Beautiful memories ache,
slipping out of reach.
I cried for my own life.

I wished I could die
at that very moment.
Everyone would cry for me.
All blames and resentments dissolve,
leaving behind gentle, tender sweetness.

Oh, it is but a dream!
Everyone will return to their own lives,
to familiar pathways.
I still have to live my own life—
beautiful for myself,
with the gifts I've been given.

When Grief Becomes Spacious

There is a song taught to us by a lay friend of Plum Village that expresses a beautiful aspiration:

Grief and love
Grief moving through me
Let my body feel the waves of love and grief

I met Jan in 2021 while she was staying with the sisters at Clarity Hamlet. She approached me quietly and asked, "Sister D, may I have some time with you?" Her whole being spoke of grief. Within a few years, she had lost her parents, her sister, and her lifelong partner. "It feels," she said, "like I died with them, yet I'm still breathing."

For years she moved through life like a shadow—working, speaking, even smiling when required, yet feeling hollow inside. Grief lived in her body: exhaustion, sleeplessness, pain, and a deep conviction that nothing mattered. Then a friend shared a quote from Thầy: "We are all the leaves of one tree. We are all the waves of one sea."

Something in her softened. She began reading more of Thầy's words and came across a line that quietly changed her days: "The best way to take care of the future is to take care of the present moment." That became her first practice. Instead of trying to survive the rest of her life, she tried to take care of just one breath, one day.

During one of her walks by the ocean, the sky flared orange and rose. She later told me, "For a moment, I felt joy—just to see the light." It was small, but it was enough to remind her that joy and sorrow can coexist.

When Jan joined a retreat on loss at one of our monasteries, each participant was invited to bring a small object representing a loved one. She placed the tokens of her parents, sister, and partner on the ancestral altar. She felt, she told me later, as though something inside finally loosened. "A great weight lifted," she said. For the first time, she could rest. She saw that holding her loved ones so tightly was also holding herself in fear. Letting go was not abandonment; it was trust.

Gradually she began to sense that those she loved had not disappeared. "They are still here," she told me later, "Just in another way." Today, Jan's grief remains, but it is spacious. She has traveled to Vietnam and visited our root temple in Hue. She writes, hikes, plays piano, and continues the practice of being present in her breath and in her body. When sorrow arises, she stops and breathes. She remembers the people she loves. She allows grief to move through her like a wave.

In that awareness, Jan has found peace—not by escaping grief, but by allowing life to bloom gently within it. She keeps walking, not rid of grief but no longer alone inside it.

Moments of Remembrance

Sometimes remembrance appears naturally in practice. At certain moments, words arise that help us stay in touch with those we love. The following two poems came during such moments—one for my beloved partner, and one for my mother.

You may wish to read them slowly, line by line, breathing gently in and out. Let each phrase guide your breath and your awareness. If you are grieving someone, breathe for them. Smile for them. If you are caring for your own body and mind, let these words remind you that to live with awareness is to die beautifully—today.

John passed away on September 25, 1999—the day before my birthday. This poem was my meditation on the fourth anniversary of his passing.

JOHN'S FOURTH-YEAR ANNIVERSARY
(SEPTEMBER 25, 2003)

This breath is for you.
This smile is for you.
This peaceful moment is for you.

I breathe for you.
I smile for you.
I cultivate this peaceful moment for you.

I am here.
I am here.
I am here.

I am here in this breath.
I am here in this smile.
I am here in this peaceful moment.

I am this breath.
I am this smile.
I am this peaceful moment.

I am life without boundaries.
You are life without boundaries.

A year later, another moment of remembrance arose, this time for my mother. This poem was my meditation the day I turned thirty-six—the same age my mother was when she disappeared from our lives.

THIRTY-SIX YEAR ANNIVERSARY

I am thirty-six years old today.
Mother, at the age of thirty-six,
You had two children,
An old husband,
Many ambitions,
Worries,
Anger,
Pain.

I am more fortunate than you—
I can take peaceful steps,
Have a chance to sit still,
No one exhausting my body.
I marvel at the autumn light.

You thought of ways to get more from life.
I ask myself: How can I stop?

Mother, my life is, because your life was.
I take these peaceful steps for you.
I sit still for you.
I heal this body for you.
The gentle light traverses infinite time.

LIVE BEAUTIFULLY, DIE BEAUTIFULLY— TODAY

Five Wishes

When we reflect on the fragile and changing nature of our lives, we may also wish to reflect on what we truly wish for, for ourselves and for those who will remain after us. One day our voice may grow quiet, our body may no longer respond, and others will carry our care forward. Taking time now to clarify our wishes is a way of meeting that reality with mindfulness, honesty, and love.

There is a simple document used in many care settings called the Five Wishes. Although it does not come from our Plum Village tradition, we can approach it in the spirit of mindfulness practice. It invites us to look deeply at how we want to live and die, how we wish to be cared for, and how we hope to be remembered.

Filling it out is not only a legal act but a spiritual one. It is a form of mindfulness—a way to look directly at our values and to express love in advance, before difficulty arises.

The Five Wishes are:

1. Who will speak for me when I cannot speak for myself.
2. What kind of care I wish to receive.
3. How I wish to be treated by others.

4. What I want my loved ones to know.
5. How I wish to be remembered.

Instead of filling it out only as a form, I invite you to sit quietly with each wish, grounded in mindful breathing and holding each question fully in awareness. You might write them down, or simply breathe with the questions:

- Who do I trust to understand my heart?
- What does "being cared for" mean to me?
- What kind of presence—my own and others'—helps me feel peaceful and at ease?
- Is there anything I wish to say now, with honesty and love, while conditions are favorable?
- How do I wish to continue in the lives of those I love?

When we contemplate these wishes, we are already preparing ourselves and our loved ones for separation with clarity and tenderness. To know our wishes is to live with fewer regrets.

You might also invite family or friends to reflect with you. Sitting together in mindful breathing, sharing from the heart, and listening deeply to one another opens compassion and deepens connection.

Ultimately, these are not documents to store away. They are living teachings. Each day that we act with understanding, speak with kindness, and love fully, we are already fulfilling our Five Wishes. Each wish we name is a seed we plant. When we live in alignment with our deepest intentions, we water those seeds daily. When we live in alignment with our deepest intentions, even the separation of death cannot divide us.

Dealing with Guilt

Our lives are made possible by a vast web of conditions—countless, interconnected causes and conditions. No single person can determine the life of another. In the same way, death and change do not arise from one isolated cause but through many conditions unfolding together. Though blame is a deeply human response, nothing has a single cause or person to blame. In times of grief, it can be natural to turn inward and place the weight of loss on ourselves. The truth is, we are not to blame for change or separation.

When I asked teenagers how they would behave differently if they truly understood that their parents' lives are impermanent, they offered thoughtful and moving responses. Many said they would spend less time online and more time with their parents. One shared that he wouldn't let temporary conflicts with parents or friends become lasting wounds that damage valuable relationships.

We can breathe now with guilt, shame, regret, and whatever painful emotions arise amid shifting conditions—meeting them with patience and compassion.

Breathing in, I'm aware that I'm feeling guilt.

Breathing out, I'm here for this emotion.

Guilt often brings a storm of emotions and accuses us of not being enough. If strong emotions arise, keep breathing with them. Hold yourself close, or gently rock back and forth. Lie face down on the earth if you need to—let Mother Earth hold you and allow any waves of emotion to move through you. Trust that they will rise and then pass.

We cannot know or prevent everything that happens (or indeed, most things that happen). In stillness and in quiet reflection, we acknowledge our limits and honor our human reality. We often believe that being "enough" is measured by what we can do, what we can say, or what we can fix. When we recognize that simply *being* has deep value—that our presence alone holds meaning—we begin to see being there for ourselves as a profound act of kindness. Because we are alive, our beloved has a chance to live on and transform through us. That, in itself, is enough.

This kind of presence can transform the way we relate to difficult emotions. Yes, we face challenges, but often it is our unfamiliarity with how to meet them—how to hold and embrace them—that makes them feel overwhelming. We can begin to practice stillness in our daily lives. Stand in silence and watch the sunset. Feel awe in the morning dew resting on the tip of a blade of grass. We can let ourselves fall in love with each single moment of beauty.

In presence, we begin to understand something deeply liberating: We are already enough.

Brother Peace: A Eulogy

During the pandemic, one of my monastic brothers, Brother Peace, experienced an unimaginable loss—both of his parents died by suicide within six months. He and his sister leaned on one another and took deep refuge in the practice and in the monastic community. What follows are his words, shared in the midst of grief and love, with his permission.

Life is not tidy. Suicide is downright messy. When I thought about what to share today, the question I asked was: "What can I say that can bring healing to me, to my family, to all of us?" I think we'll always have scars, but to the degree that we can heal, I think it will come from being able to embrace this messiness: to embrace that on one level this will never make sense and to know on another level that it does. On one hand, we will always understand how much my mom was suffering and why she did what she did, why what has happened has happened, and on the other hand, we'll never understand, not completely. On one hand, we will always feel that there was more that we could have done for my parents, and on the other hand, we know that we did everything that we could. Somehow all of this is true.

To the degree that I've been able to learn anything in the seven months since my dad's death, the insight has been around acknowledging and embracing the seeds of hopelessness and fear that lie deep in my ancestral roots, and acknowledging that my sister and I have a unique path to walk in this journey of healing and transformation. To the degree that I've learned anything in the two months since we lost our mom, it's been about coming to terms with the fact that we are not alone—understanding how big this is, how much bigger this is than my story or my family's story. My parents are in all of us. Their generosity, their friendliness, their joy; also their fear, also their sorrow. It's not just my sister's and my responsibility to take care of these seeds, it's all of our responsibility, and we will do it together.

So, what I really want to say to everyone today is to please take care of these seeds that are in all of us. Please don't suffer alone. Please know that we're all here for you. We're all doing

> *this together. Know that when you are happy and free, you're doing a lot for my sister and I, and you're doing a lot for our parents. Take care of yourselves, please, and let us help.*
>
> *And to mom and dad, I say again: We will continue these beautiful qualities that you give to us: this joy, happiness, friendship, generosity, and love. And we will transform these sorrows and this fear. We are here for you. We love you.*

In the face of unbearable loss, Brother Peace's words remind us that grief is never only personal. The Fourth Remembrance teaches that we will be separated from everyone we love, yet his eulogy also shows that love does not end with separation. It continues in the qualities we choose to carry forward, in the suffering we learn to transform, and in the way we refuse to let one another grieve alone.

Children and Loss

The loss of a beloved pet or loved one can cause a child profound pain and confusion, with effects that may last well into adulthood. For this reason, it is essential to include children in the process of illness and dying. Helping them understand what is happening, encouraging them to ask questions, responding with care and respect, and allowing them to participate in visits and caregiving when appropriate can make a significant difference. There is inherently nothing wrong with change, even when it comes in the form of illness or death and gives rise to powerful and painful emotions.

The death of a pet can be a child's first encounter with separation and loss. Sometimes the grief is just as painful as losing a beloved human. When we were children, Sonny and I had a puppy named Robin. He died suddenly just a few weeks after we brought him home. Because we had no place to bury him, we had no choice but to carry his small body to a dumpster. After that day, we never wanted another dog. The fear and pain were never spoken aloud, but they prevented us from ever considering having a pet again.

Adults often try to shield children from exposure to illness or death, especially when a parent or relative is seriously ill or has undergone drastic physical changes. Sometimes, the overwhelming demands of caregiving can also cause adults to unintentionally overlook children's emotional needs. Yet the truth is that children are deeply aware of illness and death. For example, by the age of three, my niece Sunee already showed great concern for her father's well-being. Once, as he was about to go upstairs to get a toy for her, she said, "Papa, let me do it. I don't want you to fall." Another time, while they were talking on the phone as he was driving, he dropped the phone. When he returned to the call, she asked anxiously, "What happened, Papa? Did you fall?" When Sunee was in first grade, she told me the grandmother of one of her classmates had "gone to heaven" before immediately adding, "I don't want my dad to go to heaven!"

A few years ago, a young woman came to me struggling with anorexia. As we spoke about her childhood and adolescence, she remembered how close she had been to her grandfather, who loved food and cooking. As his illness worsened and he neared death, he could no longer eat and became painfully thin. Watching this deeply distressed her, but the adults around her were so overwhelmed by the situation that they did not notice how strongly she was affected. Around that time, she began to develop a growing distaste for food that grew into revulsion.

When we allow children to learn that loss is a part of life, they are able to process fear and grief. In this way, children too come to understand that the moment before us is the one to be fully lived.

"I'm Not Comfortable!"

Children are sensitive not only to death and illness but also to harm and boundaries. My niece, Sunee, has been able to speak her mind clearly since she was a child. Sometimes, out of strong affection, I would hug her too tight. She told me, "Don't do that. I'm not comfortable." For a moment, I felt hurt, but then elated. I told her, "Sweetheart, I'm so glad you can speak up for yourself! I am proud of you!"

As a child, I didn't speak up for myself. I didn't know how. When a family member touched me inappropriately, I did not say, "Stop, don't do that. I'm not comfortable." In my child's logic, I actually felt it was my fault. I didn't know what I had done wrong, but I believed it must somehow be my fault. Sadly, many of us experience this confusion while growing up and struggle to assert control over our bodies and hold boundaries.

Sexual abuse takes place in every culture. Molesters are imagined to be evil, sick people, but the truth is they are usually our own family members, neighbors, and friends. Looking deeply into these people's lives reveals that they have often also been abused as children—the victims became the perpetrators and the cycle continues. Haunted thoughts and painful images of the abuse are rehearsed in the mind of the victim and eventually manifest as speech and bodily actions. This is one way suffering is passed on. Only when we can heal our own pain and confusion do we stop imposing them on our children and others. Whatever we cannot transform, we transmit.

As an auntie, I love my niece so much. I squeeze her or kiss her out of deep love and adoration, but this can still cause her physical pain and psychological discomfort. I'm so glad my niece told me how she felt. As adults, we need to encourage our children to express their thoughts and feelings, and to respect them. We need to listen to their child logic so we can understand what they are thinking and help them untie their internal knots. Let them know that it's not their fault when something bad happens to them or to their loved ones. Help them to not become trapped in coping mechanisms that may later become self-harming and debilitating. When children are able to speak honestly and be heard with care, healing can begin early.

A coping mechanism can be effective in the beginning, but if it becomes a habit we continue to fight internally and externally, to run away from life and relationships, or to freeze from within. Outwardly, we talk, work, and get married, but inside we are frozen. That is why it is so important for children—and for all of us—to be able to express hurt. As long as we are breathing, though, it's never too late to express these hurts to ourselves and to each other so we can recognize and transform the patterns we have carried for years. Instead of reacting automatically, we breathe and relax. If we can do this even once, we begin to break the cycle and form a mindful neural network. Slowly, a new way of being becomes possible.

Children learn what love feels like through the way we listen and respond to them. When we help them speak their truth and honor their boundaries, we protect something very precious. None of us know how long we will have together. Because separation is part of life, every moment of understanding and care becomes deeply meaningful.

The Deepest Refuge

All of us are searching for safety. We look for it in people, in places, and in the conditions of our lives. Our nervous system constantly scans the environment, asking, "Am I okay? Is everything all right?" Often, we assume safety depends on the world outside of us—other people, circumstances, and events. Yet the true source of unsafety often lies closer than we think, in the world within rather than the world outside. Our own thoughts, words, and reactions are deeply relevant to our safety. When we react impulsively or harshly, we are not safe to ourselves. Each moment of anger, fear, or blame can become a small internal war. Over time, these inner conflicts create restlessness, irritation, exhaustion, and suffering in both body and mind.

Instead of constantly scanning the outside world for danger, we can learn to turn inward and ask: "Am I safe to myself? Am I safe to others? Am I fostering safety within myself and toward those around me?" These questions invite us to take responsibility for how we relate to ourselves and those around us. Each mindful breath reminds the body and mind that we can choose a different way. Safety begins here. Remember that our time with one another is not guaranteed. The people we love will change and grow old, and one day we will no longer walk beside them in the same way. Knowing this, the way we treat one another now becomes very important. When we cultivate safety and understanding in our relationships, we create a refuge that can support us even as life continues to change.

In our daily lives, we also tend to the wounds we carry—our own and those inherited from our ancestors. We address the habits and seeds within us that harm ourselves and others. When we tend to these wounds, the pain we carry does not continue to spread to others.

Sometimes, when I hug someone, I can feel a tremor deep in their core. Often, they are not aware of it themselves, yet it is there—a subtle sign of the deep suffering many of us carry silently.

This brings us back to the teaching on interbeing: "This is in that, and that is in this." My mother was like this, so I am like this. My ancestors endured this, so I carry their legacy. The war unfolded that way, so I am a product of the Vietnam War. When we stop and look deeply, we begin to recognize the collective forces that shape our thoughts, speech, and actions until we can regard them with more equanimity and begin, bit by bit, to transform them. From the mud of suffering, lotus flowers may bloom.

One practitioner I know well speaks of how literal mud and flowers supported her healing when she was overwhelmed by the pain of separation. Her mother, with whom she cherished a close and loving relationship, died after many years of illness and intensive medical care. Though they spoke openly of all that was present and her death was blessedly peaceful—at home with a view outside, surrounded by love and holding her daughter's hand—her absence left a gaping hole in this young woman's heart.

She carried this sense of absence everywhere she went, she told me, "like a thread stitched through everything," and often felt overwhelmed by sorrow. But she had grown up deeply connected to nature and continued to seek refuge outdoors. During the years of acute grief that followed her mother's death, the spaciousness and acceptance of the natural world made it possible for her to learn to hold her own grief. Slowly, she became once more safe to herself in a world and identity that felt utterly changed after her intimately lived encounter with these Five Remembrances.

Lying under the stars and feeling the earth holding her, she could remember the truths of interbeing and impermanence in a place that felt big enough to embrace her very human reactions—our planet has, after all, accompanied humans through raw grief for thousands of years.

Over time, she began to feel the warmth of the sun as motherly love, to smell the spring flowers as the comforting scent of a home-cooked meal wafting from a familiar kitchen. She began to connect to her earthly mother in Mother Earth, and then in herself, slowly finding the ground she needed to nourish a new, wiser, and more tender way of being safe and whole.

At the same time, the absence of her mother did not disappear. There were still moments and days when the longing returned suddenly, as strong as ever. And yet, something else began to breathe alongside her grief. It was not a replacement for what was lost, but a subtle shift in how she felt her mother's presence. She began to sense her differently—woven into the earth beneath her feet, carried in the air that touched her skin, and sometimes, like a soft love inside of herself that she could offer the world because of what her mother had been and had given her. Today, pieces of earth in all its forms adorn the altar she tends at home, a reminder of her interconnection and a support for ongoing healing and grief.

Lotus flowers are fragrant, yet every part of the lotus is rooted in mud. When we understand the nature of interbeing, we take responsibility for our own healing. At the same time, we see that when we heal, we also contribute to the healing of others. This is the greatest gift of assurance and safety we can experience—a security no amount of money or social status can provide. And because one day we will inevitably be separated from one another, creating this refuge now is one of the most precious offerings we can make.

LIVE BEAUTIFULLY, DIE BEAUTIFULLY—TODAY

Creating an Altar

In Vietnamese tradition, we have a saying: "*Con cháu ở đâu, ông bà ở đó*"—"Wherever the children and grandchildren are, the grandparents are there too." This deep belief shapes our practice of establishing an altar for our deceased parents and ancestors wherever we go. An altar helps us maintain a living connection with those who have passed away. Instead of feeling only separation or loneliness, we nourish their presence and remember that we can continue to express it in our daily lives.

An altar can be as simple as a shelf mounted on the wall or a small space on top of a cabinet, especially if space is limited. It should be positioned above head height and never placed directly on the ground.

An altar typically includes a photo of the loved one, an incense urn, fresh flowers, and possibly fruits. If the family already has a collective ancestral altar, the photograph of the newly deceased may be placed beside those of earlier generations.

Lighting incense at the altar in the morning before going to work or school, and at night before bed, is a daily practice for many. In this way, the altar becomes a space for quiet reflection, meditation, or simply sharing—silently or aloud—our joys, worries, and sorrows.

To create your own altar, consider the following possibilities:

1. Find a place that feels steady and peaceful. It may be a small shelf, a table, or a quiet corner where you can pause and breathe.

2. Place a photo or symbol of your loved one. This can be a photograph, a calligraphy, or an object that reminds you of them.

3. Add a few simple offerings. Flowers, fruit, a candle, or incense can help create a sense of care and beauty.

4. Let the altar become part of your daily rhythm. You might stop there in the morning or evening to breathe quietly and reconnect.

5. Speak from the heart. Share your gratitude, your worries, or simply your presence.

6. Allow the altar to remind you how to live. Pause, breathe, and feel the quiet connection with those who have been part of your life.

Once the altar is in place, you may wish to pause, breathe softly, and offer a silent greeting to those whose lives are remembered there.

5

Our actions are our true inheritance. Our actions establish the ground on which we stand.

In the end, what remains is not what we had or who we impressed, but how we lived. Our lives are shaped by our actions—our thoughts, words, and behaviors—and we continue through them. This remembrance invites us into a deep responsibility, not as a burden but as a form of freedom. Every thought, every gesture, every word, every silence is a thread in the tapestry of our becoming and of life's unfolding after we're gone. This final remembrance offers inspiration to live with intention and care, to be faithful in the small things, and to remember that the ground we stand on is shaped not by our beliefs alone, but by the way we live. As long as we're still breathing, we have the chance to turn our thoughts toward understanding and presence. What kind of ancestor am I becoming? What trace of love will I leave behind?

Crossing a Stream

The Fifth Remembrance teaches that our actions are our true inheritance. Our actions arise from the mind we carry. If we are still carrying resentment, fear, and old stories, our actions will carry those forward as well. There's a well-known Zen story about two monks who were about to cross a deep stream. A woman asked for help, and one of the monks agreed to carry her across on his back. Once they reached the other side, he set her down and the monks continued on their way. After some time, the second monk, clearly disturbed, said to his brother, "It was not proper for you to carry that woman." The first monk calmly replied, "I put her down long ago. Why are you still carrying her?"

In the same way, we can let go of past experiences that no longer serve us. They may have been part of our journey, but they do not have to define us. There's no need to carry them forever. Practice is learning to put down what no longer needs to be carried and walking on with lightness. When we recognize this, we can let go of the weight we've been carrying and be more at ease in our bodies and minds. From that ease, our thoughts, words, and actions begin to change as well.

We all experience suffering, but we can choose not to be defined by it. When difficult emotions arise, we return to our breath and smile, recognizing them without holding on. Letting go is not forgetting; it is allowing the heart to open and flow more freely. Through this practice, we create safety within ourselves and, as a result, we can be more compassionate and become a safe person for others.

To be at home in ourselves is to be at home in the world. It's a state of being where we are safe, grounded, and open. When we rest in this inner stability, we meet life with clarity instead of fear. That, to me, is the true meaning of inner refuge. When we learn to put down what burdens us, even briefly, we touch a profound freedom and make space for a deeper seeing that naturally guides us toward the next step.

Approaching life with an open, attentive, and curious mind helps us understand more deeply how our mind works—what supports our sense of safety and happiness, and which habits or patterns of thinking may create danger or suffering for ourselves and others. When we stop carrying the weight of old narratives, old fears, old identities, we begin to walk more freely. And the steps we take in freedom—the thoughts, words, and actions we cultivate—become the inheritance we offer to the world.

Child of War, Disciple of Peace

I was born in the midst of the Vietnam War, the child of an American soldier and a Vietnamese mother. My brother and I came to the United States under the Amerasian Homecoming Act, which gave preferential immigration status to children born during the war in Vietnam from American fathers. We were placed in foster homes until we graduated from high school and became independent. Already seventeen, I worked hard to learn English and adjust to a new culture. I was determined to succeed—to prove my life could rise from the ashes of war. I studied late into the night, sometimes spending ten hours on a single chapter of biology or psychology just to grasp the vocabulary. With scholarships and the support of my professors, I made it through college and medical school.

I had thought if I could achieve enough—if I could be loved, respected, and successful—all the loss and pain of my childhood would be redeemed. Yet after my partner John's sudden death, the life I had built collapsed in an instant. I left medicine, went to Plum Village, and was ordained in 2000. I cried often in those early years, in private as well as in public. The tears came not only from despair, but also from the brutal recognition that immigration, studying hard, and ordaining as a nun had not resolved my pain. All I had tried to outrun was still there within me—my mother's absence, my father's unknown face, the sounds of war that had shaped my first breaths.

One afternoon, as I sat numbly on the edge of my bed at Deer Park Monastery, the door half-open, a great white dog walked into my room. We didn't have pets at the monastery, yet there it was—large, calm, and luminous. It sat beside me and met my gaze. I wasn't even startled; I simply looked back. After a few moments, the dog stood and left. Only then did I realize how unusual the dog's presence was. I immediately stepped outside to look for it. To my bewilderment, the courtyard was completely silent and empty. To this day, I don't know if that dog was real or not. Perhaps the spirit of the mountain that rises behind the monastery came to remind me that life remains mysterious and mighty even when I fail to see it.

War leaves its traces in the body and the mind. It lives on in the way we breathe, the way we react, the way we love or withhold love. Miraculously, mindfulness enables us to look deeply into those traces. We do not erase them but transform them into understanding. When I breathe with awareness, I also breathe for my mother and father, for all who could not breathe freely. When I walk in peace, I also walk for those who never had such a chance.

After settling in Deer Park Monastery and other Plum Village practice centers in the US for eighteen years, I returned to Plum Village again in 2022, just a few months after Thầy's passing. The occasion marked my twenty-second year as a nun. So many beautiful memories returned: Thầy walking slowly between the rows of trees, his gentle laughter at the sound of a bird, his presence like sunlight after rain. The monastery was filled with young people—over four hundred had come for the Wake Up retreat. I felt deep happiness to see the community continue to thrive after Thầy's passing. Even deeper was the quiet joy of returning to a place where I had suffered so deeply twenty-two years earlier and now discovering stability and ease in myself.

Each of us carries the continuation of our ancestors: their wounds, their fears, their resilience, their hopes. To live mindfully is to honor that inheritance and to transform it. It is how we make peace real, not as an idea but as a daily act of remembrance and renewal. I hear the whisper of all who came before me: "Live gently. Live beautifully. You are the continuation of countless lives that wanted peace." Breathing in, I touch this truth. Breathing out, I smile. I am home in myself. I am home in the world. And when we begin to feel at home in ourselves, we also begin to see ourselves more clearly in others.

Seeing Ourselves in Each Other

As we learn to put things down—as in the Zen story of the monk who carried the woman across the river—we begin to notice how much the world invites us to pick things back up again: suspicion, fear, resentment, and division.

During times of turbulence or social upheaval, perhaps the most important refuge we can cultivate is inner stillness. When the world pulls us toward sides, toward arguments, toward the narrowing of the heart, we can ground ourselves again in the simple truth of interbeing: "In the white, there is the black. In the black, there is the white." None of us exists independently. Every one of us is shaped by countless conditions—family, society, culture, history—and every action we take affects others, even those we will never meet.

When we forget this, we become isolated, suspicious, and afraid. When we remember it, gratitude and compassion return. A heart that holds compassion can know happiness, for it calls our attention to the people and conditions that nurture and support us every moment.

At times, we grow complacent, overlooking the very conditions that safeguard us: our family, our community, our practice, and our friendships. Awareness of all that is holding us helps us take better care of them.

Experiences of racial, gender, or religious discrimination can trigger the body even before the mind understands what is happening. Instead of engaging these topics only at the level of emotion or ideology, our practice guides us back to the body—to feel directly how anger, fear, pain, and defensiveness take shape within us. This is a return to the first establishment of mindfulness—awareness of the body in the body. When we notice tightness, shaking, burning, or heat, we can breathe with it and let our body calm and soften before doing anything else. Only then can empathy and understanding arise.

This is how we become a refuge: not by ignoring suffering in the world, not by drowning in it, but by meeting it with a steady body and a capacious mind. By caring for our own reactivity, we create safety not only for ourselves but also for those around us. When we remember interbeing, we cannot cast others out of our hearts—not even those who think or look different from us. We learn to see ourselves in them, and them in us.

And each time we return to the breath, each time we choose to calm our body before speaking or acting, we contribute a small drop of peace into the collective stream of our world, which continues long after our bodies have returned to the earth.

Taking Refuge in Oneself

The Fifth Remembrance reveals that our actions are our true inheritance, truly the ground we stand upon. If that ground feels unsteady, if we fear disappearing after we are gone, it is because we have forgotten how to come home to ourselves.

I once watched a documentary about human trafficking that revealed something both heartbreaking and instructive. A trafficker described how he would approach a young woman and say, "Your eyes are beautiful." If she smiled and thanked him, he would walk away. But if she looked down and denied it, he knew he could manipulate her and groom her to be trafficked.

The story stayed with me for a long time. It revealed something painful but true: People often prey upon those who do not feel safe within themselves. When we doubt our worth, the world can sense it. Yet when we stand in quiet confidence—when we know we belong to ourselves—it becomes much harder for others to trap us.

This is why the practice of taking refuge in ourselves is so important. It is not selfishness or isolation. It is learning to become a safe place within our own body and mind. I didn't know this kind of mindfulness practice when I was a teenager, so now I do my best to share it with others—especially young people. Learning to be present with ourselves is a powerful form of self-regulation—the ability to pause, breathe, and respond instead of reacting automatically.

Many of us try to soothe our pain in ways that do not truly help—through distraction, through substances, through endless activity. We reach for games, social media, cigarettes, alcohol, drugs, sex, or work. These are attempts to comfort ourselves when we do not yet know how to come home to our own breath and body.

Taking refuge within is how we come home and steady the earth beneath our own feet. It is the simple art of pausing, noticing, and choosing a kinder next step. We stop scattering ourselves and return to the breath, to the body, and to what we can care for while we're still here. In doing so, we become a refuge for ourselves, and naturally, for others.

With practice, we can learn to relate differently to our suffering. We can even become a kind soulmate to our own addictions and pain. Instead of fighting them or feeling ashamed, we greet them with curiosity, asking questions and learning from them. We ask for their help and speak to them gently: "I know you tried to protect me in your own way, but let's find a different path now."

In a spiritual life, we learn to self-regulate in a more mindful, loving way by coming back to the breath and by taking mindful steps. This calms both mind and body and reconnects them. It's a way of saying to ourselves: "I am here for you. You are safe with me." When we speak to ourselves harshly, we become our own abuser. When we treat ourselves with gentleness and compassion, we begin to feel safer in the world, to establish a steady ground from which we can live.

Remind yourself of your own aspirations. Remember what you love, what you care about. Recall the positive conditions still present in your life. Give yourself another chance, and another and another. Because, my dear ones, we all deserve mercy. We all deserve compassion. We all deserve understanding, forgiveness, transformation, and healing.

This safety is not abstract. It shapes the way we move in the world. It shapes the relationships we enter, the boundaries we hold, and the choices we make. I know many teen girls—and older women as well—who stay in toxic relationships because they're afraid that if they leave, no one will love them. Men also fall into this pattern of unworthiness. When we accept mistreatment, we silently tell the world: "I do not believe I am worthy of love. I'm up for auction. I place myself at your mercy." But you are worthy.

You have always been worthy.

True love begins with self-care, self-respect, and compassion—for ourselves and for others. When we take refuge in ourselves, we no longer chase after love as something to be exchanged, earned, or proven. We are our own safe harbor, our own soulmate. Our own way of being is love itself.

The heart of self-regulation through mindfulness is learning to be at home in our own presence—learning to be the one who can hold our pain, our breath, our trembling body, and whisper, "Stay with me. You are safe here." The trafficker in that documentary understood something tragic: People who feel unworthy can be easily trapped. When we can love ourselves into this calm harbor and breathe ourselves back to belonging, we become much harder to manipulate or control. No cruel thought, no unkind world can claim us. We are already home.

Wholeness

For many years, I carried the belief that I wasn't good enough—that somehow, I wasn't enough. There was a deep emptiness within me, a kind of vacuum that nothing seemed to fill. Many adults, no matter how successful we appear, carry this same bottomless feeling inside.

One way we begin to soften that feeling is by learning to feel awe again—an awe we often lose as we grow older. As children, wonder comes so easily. We can spend hours looking at the sky, watching insects, or studying the way sunlight touches the floor. This natural intimacy with life fades when we become busy or burdened, but the magic hasn't gone anywhere.

A drop of sunlight on the floor, a flower blooming in winter, passion fruit ripening in the garden—each remains a quiet wonder. Mindfulness helps us reconnect with this magic by opening our eyes, our hearts, and our minds to what has been here all along. Reconnecting with wonder, we start to remember that life is already offering us so much, and that we ourselves are full of delights.

Slowly, the heaviness inside begins to soften. Through the steady practice of mindful breathing and Beginning Anew with my wounded inner child, I gradually began to open my heart and receive love and care, not only from others but from myself. These days, I no longer speak unkindly to myself. Even when I make mistakes, I don't spiral into self-criticism. Instead, I gently say to myself, "I'm sorry. I'll try again." After many years of this, a quiet thought arose from within: "I am enough. I am whole."

It was simple, yet profoundly empowering.

How do we move from a state of emptiness to a sense of wholeness? Gradually, the sense of lack that once seemed so solid begins to dissolve. What once felt like a hole becomes spaciousness.

When we learn to be our own soulmate, to be a true refuge for ourselves, the old feeling of not being enough begins to release. There are no longer barriers or separation—just openness, boundless love, and peace. To be a soulmate to ourselves is to care for our body, our breath, our feelings, our thoughts, our perceptions, and the tender places within us that long for understanding and acceptance.

In Vietnamese, the word for soulmate, *tri kỷ*, carries this meaning beautifully. "Tri" means to remember, to know, to take care of, and to master. "Kỷ" means oneself. A soulmate is not someone we search for outside of us. As spiritual practitioners, we have the precious opportunity to become our own soulmates—to be present for what was, what is, and what will be.

Feeling whole allows us to see more clearly what helps us and what harms us. From this place of inner safety, we can examine our attachments, reactions, and patterns with honesty and steadiness. Clinging begins to fall away. We stop chasing someone else to complete us. We realize we already have everything we need at this moment. From this place of clarity and safety, we can love others with far greater freedom and joy—without grasping, without fear, without losing ourselves. Loving-kindness becomes an effortless extension of wholeness: "May I be safe. May I choose happiness. May I be a source of peace and joy for myself and others." These simple aspirations are not wishes but recognitions of what is already possible. When we live from this place of wholeness, our thoughts, words, and actions begin to reflect it naturally.

Presence Is Protection

If we don't know how to take care of our mental formations—anger, fear, and despair—we may cause more harm and suffering in the world. I often ask young people, When you see all the discrimination and violence in the world, how do you take care of what arises inside you? One day you will become adults: teachers, doctors, lawmakers, parents, and leaders. The question is not only what kind of world you will inherit, but what kind of world you are already shaping through your actions today. Will you respond differently and help protect others, or will you tread the same path as those currently in positions of power and authority? What are you doing now? The future begins with what you do now.

During a conversation on Zoom during the pandemic, some young people shared that they comfort their friends of color, telling them, "It will be okay." Anti-Asian sentiment was strong at the time, and we discussed how to include and protect each other. One teen said, "If I see someone sitting alone at school, I'll invite them to join me, to be my friend." These are small, yet powerful ways we can nurture life, appreciation, and healing in our daily lives. Protection does not always appear as grand gestures. Often it begins with something very simple: noticing someone's pain and choosing not to turn away.

It may be easy to blame others—"The Chinese spread the virus," "The white people did this," "The Black people did that"—but the truth is, "they" are in "us." If we do not take care of our own fear, anger, and prejudice, those same forces continue to move through the world. But presence is not passive. When we are truly present, we notice suffering sooner, and we respond differently. When we learn to recognize and calm reactivity within ourselves, our presence protects ourselves and others.

Releasing Attachment

During Thầy's 2011 US tour, I confided in Thầy at his cabin in Colorado, "I feel deeply fortunate to be happy in my practice and able to serve others. Yet I still sense a lingering desire I cannot seem to let go of. I continue to long for a special person in my life."

I'm grateful I could always be open and honest with Thầy. In response to my admission, Thầy said, "You cannot catch fish with two hands. You can't be a doctor and an artist at the same time." This Vietnamese proverb means that you cannot pursue multiple goals or roles simultaneously and expect to succeed in all of them. At that moment, I saw that part of my suffering came from trying to hold on to two lives at once—one of complete dedication to the path, and one of clinging to a fantasy of romantic fulfillment.

For many years, I didn't truly want that feeling of attraction to go away, because it brought novelty and excitement. When I became sick with Lyme disease, I began looking more deeply into my beliefs about attachment and relationship. I felt an aspiration growing to let go of the grasping that never brought me happiness. When John died, I thought I would die too. I was so desperate, surely because I loved him, surely because he was my soulmate, but also because his death shattered all hopes and illusions I carried: that if I became successful and found a loving partner, my past suffering would somehow be compensated. Yet nothing guaranteed that. I wasn't happy, even though I was a doctor. I had a loving, faithful, wonderful partner, and then he suddenly disappeared. Another person, I knew, would not be the answer to my happiness. Slowly, painfully, I realized I had to learn to be my own soulmate.

My monastic life has taught me to cherish my body and my life as my own soulmate. When pain arises, I have learned to stop all actions and truly be present with my body and my pain. I tell myself, "I am here for you. I love you." I used to daydream and grasp at things outside of myself. When I looked at the moon, I saw my beloved. When I looked at the flower, I saw my beloved. When I ate something good, I thought of my beloved. I truly believed that if I let go of attachment, my life would be hollow.

Thầy shared that when he was young, he went through a period of deep attachment to a nun, and when it was "over," he felt completely light and at ease. There was a time when I woke each morning feeling unbearably heavy, hardly able to breathe, while sadness and a dull, aching sorrow lingered over me all day. I kept praying, "Please let me choose peace. Please let me choose freedom." I held on to my breath and my steps, doing my best to follow the community's daily schedule.

Then one morning I woke with the awareness that my very first breath felt gentle and pleasant, my chest light, and the space around me vast. "Has it already passed? Was that all?" I asked myself in amazement. The truth is, when attachment passes, what remains is what is truly here: the blue sky, warm sunshine, flowers stretching their petals and proudly saying, "Here I am. I am alive!"

My spiritual practice has gradually trained me to dwell in the present moment as it is. Now, when I look at the moon, I simply see the moon. When I look at the flower, I see the flower. When I eat a bowl of soup, I enjoy it fully! My beloved is no longer an object to grasp. Releasing dualistic thinking, I already have everything.

So, I choose to be a practitioner many times each day. When the wish for peace is present, peace naturally follows. To have a path, to have the freedom to choose, is true happiness.

This is a poem I wrote in a moment of feeling deep peace and freedom:

For so many years
I yearned for you
I thought of you each
and every day

in the midst of busyness
in the midst of solitude

A thought of you would arise
like something dropped

suddenly
into a deep, hollow well

Reverberating
        stirring
        unquenchable

Now there is no thought of you
and I am glad
There is no yearning for you
and I am thankful

I can just be
with what is
        simply be.

It took me nineteen years of practice to reach this point of no longer feeling the gnawing need to grasp or cling to anything or anyone. Now, when I look at the moon, I simply see the moon. When I look at the flower, I see the flower. And that is enough.

LIVE BEAUTIFULLY, DIE BEAUTIFULLY— TODAY

Enoughness

Recently, a young man told me that after hearing my talk on being enough, he and his two siblings decided to get a tattoo of the Chinese character for "enough" (足). His tattoo is on his right bicep, his brother's on his thigh, and his sister's on her calf. He pulled out a photo of the three of them proudly showing their tattoos. Smiling, I teased, "But do you really practice it?" He answered, "That's exactly why I got the tattoo—to remind myself I am enough."

Many of us struggle with the feeling of "not being enough." We often equate our sense of inadequacy with a lack of abundance in our lives. Interestingly, the Chinese character for "enough" (which is also the character for "foot") incorporates symbols for a mouth, a vertical line for the body, a horizontal line for an arm, and two legs. Simply having a mouth, a body, an arm, and two legs qualifies us as already being enough!

Whether our head is large or small, our body slender or stout, our limbs long or short—we are enough, just as we are. It is true happiness to realize this profound truth.

This daily meditation can nourish our sense of enoughness. Please adapt it to fit your own body and abilities.

Breathing in, I am aware that I am still breathing in.
Breathing out, I am aware that I am still breathing out.
Still breathing in, still breathing out—that's enough!

Breathing in, I am aware that I still have my head.
Breathing out, I am aware that I can still learn and gain insights.
Still have my head—that's enough!

Breathing in, I am aware that I still have a mouth.
Breathing out, I am aware that I can speak lovingly, smile, kiss my loved ones, and savor the pleasure of chewing food with a full set of teeth!
Still have my mouth—that's enough!

Breathing in, I am aware that I still have a body.
Breathing out, I am aware that I can sit, walk, run, dance, and do many things comfortably and effortlessly!
Still have a body—that's enough!

Breathing in, I am aware I still have two arms—or even just one.
Breathing out, I feel them alive and functional.

Still have two arms—or one—that's enough!

Breathing in, I am aware that I still have two legs.
Breathing out, I feel them healthy and strong.
Still have two legs—that's enough!

Breathing in, I am aware that I have more than enough conditions to be happy.
Breathing out, I am aware that I am more than enough!
I have enough! I am enough!

Enoughness in an Age of Addiction and AI

We live in an age of acceleration, where craving is both the currency and the wound. When we forget that we are already enough, just as we are, the mind begins searching endlessly for something more. Whether it's a drink, a movie, or a thought that keeps spinning in our minds, the mechanism is the same: We reach outward in an attempt to flee our suffering.

Often, this results in an addiction—sometimes obvious, sometimes subtle. The Buddha called this "thirst." He also taught that by turning toward thirst with awareness, we can find freedom right where the craving begins.

When I recently asked a group of young people at our annual Teens Camp at Deer Park if they would rather be popular than be loved, no one raised their hand. When I asked if they would rather have a few true friends than many superficial acquaintances, most hands went up.

We long for genuine, meaningful friendships, but here's the paradox: We often pour our time into social media, connecting with people—mostly strangers—who add little to our peace or joy. It's important to check in with ourselves: Are we acting in ways that truly align with our values? Are we living authentically?

Elon Musk once remarked, "You are all cyborgs, you just don't realize it." In many ways, it's true: We spend hours each day tethered to screens, half-human, half-machine. For young people, the question grows sharper. A mother once asked me to counsel her son, who had refused to continue his education, announcing, "AI is going to take over the world of knowledge. Why should I go to college? I should just start a business and make money."

Trying to compete with artificial intelligence is a losing game. A supercomputer can learn in seconds what humans take years to absorb. ChatGPT can transcribe, translate, and even compose poems at speeds far beyond human capacity. If we see learning and living as a competition with machines, we will always lose—and we will undoubtedly suffer. The way forward is not to outsmart AI, but to grow more deeply human. Technology will advance; that is certain. Authenticity—our ability to be real, to love and be loved, to discover ourselves, to be truly free—is what sets us apart as living beings.

Too often, we measure ourselves against others and now even against the capabilities of machines—and come up short. The truth is simpler: We are already enough. When illness or limitation touches us, certain capacities remain intact: to walk, to smile, to use the restroom independently, to embrace a child, to accompany the dying. Forgetting this sufficiency can lead us into numbing patterns of escapism, addiction, and self-sabotage.

This is the second arrow, our denial and flight, which exponentially multiplies suffering. The invitation is to choose another way. Breathing in, we remember we already have enough conditions to be happy. We are enough. Breathing out, we aspire to take good care of our circumstances, inside ourselves and in the world.

In a world increasingly shaped by machines, to live authentically is a radical act. It is how we become true ancestors, human beings whose presence cannot be outsourced or replaced. To live with enoughness in this age means to meet our insecurity and cravings not with fear or denial, but with authentic insight and steady presence.

Right Diligence

When we begin to see how craving and comparison shape our lives, the question naturally arises: What can we do with these habits? The Buddha offered a very practical answer: Right Diligence. Right Diligence, a part of the Noble Eightfold Path, is the art of choosing what we nourish. It is divided into four aspects. At any moment, our mind is like a garden. Seeds of anger, fear, joy, compassion, and craving all lie within us. The first two aspects of Right Diligence focus on cultivating the positive seeds already present within us. When we experience suffering, including from illness, grief, or addiction, it's easy to focus only on the negative in our situation and in ourselves. However, we all have positive seeds—seeds of joy, love, understanding, kindness, generosity, and well-wishes for ourselves and others. The practice is to nurture these wholesome seeds, no matter how small they might seem at the moment. Recognize them, acknowledge them, water them, invite them to grow and stay longer in your consciousness.

Sometimes these seeds appear as the wounded child within us. When you notice your inner child—in your thoughts, speech, or behaviors—acknowledge them with a gentle greeting: "Hello, I see you! Help me care for you." Invite your inner child to remain for a while; get to know each other, and nurture seeds of gratitude for each other.

The other two aspects of Right Diligence focus on the negative seeds of craving, self-doubt, shame, guilt, blame, sadness, and so on. When they arise, acknowledge them without judgment, and invite them to gently return to your store consciousness. Breathe, relax your body, and let any waves of emotion settle. Avoid rehearsing negative patterns with thoughts, movies, music, games, conversations, drugs, or places that reinforce them. The practice is to refrain from watering these negative seeds by getting triggered or ruminating on them. Only when the emotional intensity has calmed can we examine these seeds with clarity and understanding.

This approach resonates with recovery traditions such as the Twelve-Step program, which also invites us to recognize suffering honestly and walk toward healing one step at a time. Through training in Right Diligence, we cultivate wholesome seeds and the capacity for understanding, love, and tolerance so when challenges arise, we are not swept away by our survival instincts. With mindfulness practice, we can draw on calmness, wisdom, and equanimity.

Sycamore

Recently, a beautiful woman came to Deer Park on a Day of Mindfulness. She introduced herself as Sycamore and thanked me for my book *Healing: Journey from Doctor to Nun*. When we embraced, I felt her whole body trembling, as though she were shaking deep inside. From experience, I recognized that she was carrying the weight of trauma.

I invited her to take a short walk with me, and afterward we sat together in silence before she began to speak. Sycamore was in a rehabilitation program for addiction. She had found my book in the center's library, checked it out, and read it slowly each evening. The book brought her comfort and reminded her that healing was still possible. Her rehabilitation program allowed participants to listen to Dharma talks on YouTube and to read works by Thich Nhat Hanh and the Plum Village monastics, and she said hearing Thầy's voice made her feel less alone.

As we talked, I could sense her gratitude—not only for the teachings, but for the chance to speak openly about her experience. Addiction carries deep stigma and silent shame. And yet, even in this cycle of suffering, the seed of awakening is still there, waiting to be tended. To share her journey without fear of judgment was already a form of healing.

Sycamore told me she had begun practicing mindful breathing after hearing a Dharma talk online. "At first," she said, "it felt impossible—my breath was so short, it almost hurt to pay attention." We spoke about how difficult it can be to return to the body after years of alienation. I shared a simple practice: to let the hands open and close gently with the breath.

Breathing in, I gently close my hands.

Breathing out, I gently open them.

Breathing in, I quietly befriend my in-breath.

Breathing out, I quietly befriend my out-breath.

Slowly, the mind comes home to the body. Slowly, the body remembers safety.

I told Sycamore befriending our breath is an act of love—a way of saying hello to ourselves after years of harsh judgment and self-condemnation. Addiction often becomes part of our identity: I'm an addict. I'm ruined. I'm a failure. I'm worthless. Our practice teaches that we are never only the things that have harmed us.

Many who struggle with addiction have lost trust in others—and, more painfully, in themselves. Family members may withdraw their support. Work, marriage, and stability crumble. The body bears the cost through withdrawal, exhaustion, anxiety, and depression. Suddenly, the storm feels endless.

But healing begins the moment we touch pain with kind awareness. Recovery is never only about abstaining. It is about awakening—returning, again and again, to what is real and alive within us. This is where true transformation begins, transformation that changes the way we think and live.

Understanding and Healing

Traditionally, the Eightfold Path begins with Right View, because the mind is the painter of everything we see and experience. It is the mind that shapes how we meet the world, how we hold our grief and pain, and whether we are able to heal from it. Our ability to heal depends on the quality of our mind. Whether we live a full, meaningful life or remain trapped in suffering is determined by the way we relate to our experience and how we choose to respond. When views are grounded in interbeing, we recognize that the one who has caused harm also carries suffering, and the one who suffers has, at times, caused harm. With this understanding, we no longer identify solely as victims. Instead, we take a compassionate and responsible stance toward our lives and the lives of others. We invest our energy not in blame, but in transformation, trusting that healing is possible within us and around us.

We may go through a rehab program once, twice, or even many times. It's easy to feel weighed down by the thought, "I failed before; what's different now?" Real courage is the willingness to begin again—to actively seek the conditions and community that nourish healing.

The most powerful factor in changing the brain is the mind itself. To change the mind is to change the brain. Neuroplasticity arises through the Eightfold Path, which includes the cultivation of Right Mindfulness, Right Concentration, Right View, and Right Thinking. These, in turn, give rise to Right Effort, Right Speech, Right Action, and Right Livelihood. Each aspect of the living ground of this path inter-is with the others, nourishing and sustaining each other.

Thoughts arise constantly, often without our awareness. With mindfulness, we can see them clearly and ask: Is this thought wholesome or unwholesome? We breathe in, breathe out, and we smile to a painful thought. We can even speak to it gently: "I love you. I'm here for you. Let's give each other another chance."

When shame or disgust toward our body arises, we can meet it differently: "Thank you for being here, dear body. Thank you for your resilience and forgiveness. Help me love you and care for you well." In this way, Right View and Right Thinking become the foundation for our transformation. They lead to Right Speech—first toward ourselves, then toward others—and to Right Actions that nurture our body and the world it lives in with kindness and appreciation.

I often encourage young people to massage their faces, hold their own hands, or hug themselves when anxiety or withdrawal arise. Body and mind are not separate entities—the tremor of the body is often the cry of the wounded mind. We learn to soothe ourselves with tenderness, rocking gently as we breathe, whispering words of care. These small acts of presence restore trust in ourselves and in life.

Healing begins in the simple willingness to stay—to breathe, to notice, to love what is still trembling inside us. When we return to our breath with understanding, we are already on the path of recovery. Every mindful breath, every gentle thought, every act of care is a quiet revolution against despair—a way of remembering that the capacity for healing always lives within us.

Five Aspirations for an Age of AI

If our actions are our continuation, then the question becomes: How do we live in a way that continues wisely? If we wish to live with authentic insight and true love in this age of artificial intelligence, we need clear ground beneath our feet—guiding principles that help us stay human amid constant change. Thầy called these principles the Five Mindfulness Trainings—a modern expression of the Buddha's ancient ethical path. Here, I offer a condensed version of them simply as living aspirations that help us remember what continues through us when everything else changes. For the full version, please see the Plum Village website.[14]

We become human through what we care for and through the care we offer again and again. What we give our attention to shapes our continuation. Artificial intelligence can process information, but it cannot love, suffer, or awaken. Only humans can do that. The Five Mindfulness Trainings help us protect this precious capacity. They are not rules, but reminders—directions we can choose so our thoughts, words, and actions may be life-giving. Practiced in this spirit, the Five Mindfulness Trainings bring the Fifth Remembrance to life: My actions are my true continuation. What follows is not a code of behavior, but five aspirations for living beautifully—and continuing beautifully—in a changing world.

The First Mindfulness Training

Reverence for Life

Aware of the suffering caused by harm and violence, I aspire to protect life in all its forms—human, animal, plant, and mineral—beginning with my own.

Reverence for life begins close to home. It begins in how we speak to ourselves, how we breathe, how we treat this body that carries us. When we repeatedly think, "I'd rather be dead," we plant a seed of harm. When we place a hand on the body and say, "I'm here for you," we plant a seed of care.

This body ages moment by moment. Our actions toward life within and around us create the world we will leave behind. Reverence means not postponing care or waiting until our strength is gone to honor beauty. When we care for life now, while we still can, we age, change, and let go with love.

The Second Mindfulness Training

True Happiness

Aware that chasing wealth, stimulation, and approval often deepens suffering, I aspire to cultivate happiness rooted in understanding, generosity, and enoughness.

True happiness is not something we wait for, but something we practice. Each time we choose what nourishes rather than what numbs, we shape our continuation. Fragility and change are part of life. True happiness does not mean avoiding pain, but living in such a way that even when the body falters, the mind remains steady. When we practice generosity and joy, we strengthen the medicine already within us. When we consume food, media, conversations, work, thoughts, and views mindfully, we protect not only our own well-being, but the well-being of those who will come after us.

The Third Mindfulness Training

True Love

Aware that desire is not the same as love, I aspire to care for my relationships with honesty, responsibility, and tenderness.

True love is not built on intensity alone, but on trust, presence, and care over time. It begins with how we speak to ourselves. When we learn to treat our own inner child with kindness, we no longer need to harm ourselves—or others—in the name of love.

Love practiced this way becomes a continuation of safety, dignity, and compassion. To love is to know we can lose. We are of the nature to die, and so are those we love. True love cherishes without clinging. It becomes the kind of presence that does not need forever to leave a beautiful trace.

The Fourth Mindfulness Training

Loving Speech and Deep Listening

Aware that words can heal or harm long after they are spoken, I aspire to speak and listen in ways that reduce suffering and restore connection.

In our tradition, we do not "strike" the bell during mindfulness practice—we invite it. This gentle language reminds us that every word carries weight. What we say becomes part of the world. What we listen to becomes part of us. When we pause, breathe, and speak with care, we change the direction of our continuation. Even the ones we speak with every day are changing. Relationships shift. Understanding deepens or fades. When we speak and listen with care, we build bridges strong enough to hold the changes that will surely come.

The Fifth Mindfulness Training

Nourishment and Healing

Aware that what I consume becomes my body and my mind, I aspire to nourish myself in ways that support clarity, steadiness, and healing.

This includes what we eat, what we watch, what we listen to, what we touch, and what we repeatedly think. When we consume to escape loneliness or pain, suffering grows. When we return to the present moment—to breath, body, and connection—we begin to heal. To nourish ourselves wisely is to nourish the world we will continue into.

Taken together, these Five Aspirations remind us that our love and freedom are not abstract, but are lived through our daily choices. Each thought, each word, each action is already our continuation. To live in this way is to remain human in an age of machines—to let awareness, compassion, and responsibility be what survives us.

LIVE BEAUTIFULLY, DIE BEAUTIFULLY— TODAY

Touching My Continuation

To begin, return to your breath—gently, simply. In this moment, there is nothing you need to fix or force. Only this breath and the seeds it waters.

Breathing in, I am aware of the thoughts I am cultivating.

Breathing out, I recognize these thoughts will be my continuation.

Breathing in, I am aware of the words I am about to speak.

Breathing out, I see how my words will continue in others.

Breathing in, I touch the actions I am about to take today.

Breathing out, I choose to let my actions be rooted in understanding and love.

Breathing in, I see the seeds I want to water—patience, compassion, clarity.

Breathing out, I am determined to water them today.

Breathing in, I touch the impermanence of this very breath.

Breathing out, I touch the truth that I will grow old, fall ill, and die.

Breathing in, I vow to live so that my love continues beautifully.

Breathing out, I choose to live beautifully and die beautifully each day.

As the practice comes to a close, allow yourself to rest in the depth of your aspiration. You do not need to hurry or change anything right away. Simply trust that each mindful breath nurtures a real and steady seed. Your thoughts, your words, and your actions become a beautiful continuation of the person you wish to be—today, and in all the days that follow.

Our True Continuation

Even great people die, but their ideals, their aspirations, and their actions live on. Every life leaves traces. Some fade quickly; others last for generations, carried forward by a single moment of kindness, clarity, or courage. In the Buddha's teaching, this continuation is called "karma." Karma is not fate or retribution, but action and the ongoing life of each action. We often use the word "karma" casually—"instant karma," we say when someone faces quick consequences. Yet "karma," in Sanskrit, simply means action—of mind, speech, or body—and the results that follow. What we offer the world returns to us: Kindness invites kindness; anger begets anger. Our thoughts, speech, and deeds do not end; they ripple outward, shaping our families, our communities, and the world long after we are gone. In this web of interbeing, our happiness is never private. It is a shared energy that nourishes everyone it touches.

Through practice, we cultivate the understanding that when we pause to breathe before speaking, when we choose generosity over judgment, happiness over despair, we plant seeds that will blossom into the future. We don't need to wait for another lifetime to see our continuation. It is alive in every thought we nurture, every word we choose, every step we take.

In Vietnam, my grandmother supported Venerable Đồng Châu in many ways, including giving him money to help him escape in the 1980s. He did not succeed in leaving, and he later became a highly respected monk. He was the monk present with my grandmother for her last breaths.

Decades later, I was visiting my family in Vietnam and found myself in urgent need of money to help my cousin get dentures. Out of desperation, I considered borrowing the Sangha's funds—which I was supposed to bring back to Deer Park—but I had no idea how I would repay the $2,000.

Just hours before I was to leave for the airport, Venerable Đồng Châu came to see me. He handed me $2,000 and said my grandmother had given him money forty years ago, and now he was returning it. I cried as I accepted his money with both hands. I gave the entire amount to my cousin. At that moment, both my cousin and I reaped the fruit of my grandmother's generosity four decades earlier! Karma always finds its way home—sometimes across oceans, sometimes across generations.

Thầy's Presence

Thầy had a profound capacity to be truly present for the person in front of him. Whenever you were with him, it felt as if you were the only person in the world. You felt special—genuinely seen and heard. Thầy didn't rely on charisma or outward charm; his presence came from deep, continuous practice. His way of being was so genuine and generous, his love so real.

I remember one occasion when another sister and I brought food to our teacher at his hermitage, not far from our nunnery. Thầy always insisted we eat with him, so we brought extra food for ourselves. As we were finishing the meal, Thầy began to cut and peel an apple, carefully offering each piece. When one piece fell to the ground, he quietly picked it up, set it aside, and continued peeling. Thầy handed the clean pieces to us, and then, with a gentle smile, carved the dropped piece and ate it himself.

That moment humbled me deeply. Our teacher chose to give us the best and keep what had fallen for himself. An insight arose in me: Thầy is a human being, just like all of us. He, too, has known suffering and habits. Through diligent practice, he transformed them so he could offer the very best of himself to his students, whether monastic or lay.

That small piece of apple became symbolic of Thầy's life to me. He had worked on himself, for himself, and for all of us. Every moment with him, whether at the airport or while sharing a piece of fruit, was a transmission. Each interaction was an invitation to experience mindfulness, kindness, and the deep interconnectedness of life.

Meeting Thầy's Life Force

After Thầy's stroke in 2014, which left him hemiplegic and unable to speak, I had the opportunity to visit him at his root temple, Từ Hiếu, in March 2019. Thầy was eating breakfast when I walked in. He looked at me intently as I knelt with joined palms. "Dear Thầy, I am Dang Nghiem, your child and disciple," I said. Thầy smiled and nodded several times. I settled on the floor by his feet as Thầy returned to his breakfast. Thầy could no longer speak due to the stroke, but he looked into my eyes with his Zen Master's penetrating gaze, and I smiled brightly in return. It seemed Thầy was checking, "Are you here?" and my smile confirmed, "Yes, I am absolutely here!" At one point, Thầy held out his left hand to me. I held Thầy's hand with both of mine. I closed my eyes and breathed mindfully as I felt the softness and warmth emanating from his hand. The stillness in our connection was profound.

Thầy ate each morsel of food slowly and mindfully, closing his eyes while chewing. Although his food was puréed, Thầy took around forty-five minutes to finish each meal. There was much wisdom in Thầy's mindful eating: It helped him enjoy his food and prevent him from aspirating and getting pneumonia. While Thầy ate, one brother sat on his right to assist. At least two or three sisters also ate with Thầy. The two sisters who cooked that day stopped by to see how Thầy liked the food and to decide what to cook for his next meal. A group of about twenty-four monastic brothers and sisters took turns caring for Thầy. The sisters cooked, and the brothers attended to Thầy's needs. Day or night, every gesture Thầy made was acknowledged and responded to by his group of attendants. Deep love and affection flowed between teacher and disciples. These brothers and sisters cared for Thầy with so much joy, attentiveness, and tenderness that I cried out of gratitude, happiness, and reassurance. The transmission continued uninterrupted.

One morning, some of us sisters decided to make lotus tea for Thầy. To mark the occasion, we each playfully donned gigantic lotus leaves like wide-brim hats and organized a small procession past Thầy's window with a bouquet of lotus buds in each of our arms. Thầy watched us with interest and amusement. Settling outside his room, we filled each lotus bud with black tea leaves, wrapped the bouquets in lotus leaves, and placed the stems in a bucket of water. Then the whole bucket was left in the freezer so that the tea had time to fully absorb the lotus fragrance.

At one point, the attendant brought Thầy to the door in his wheelchair to watch. I was afraid Thầy could not see well through the glass, so I cracked the door open and asked, "Would a sister bring a lotus bud closer for Thầy to see?" Immediately, I felt his hand on my right elbow. His clutch was sudden, firm, and powerful, like lightning! It was a moment of profound stopping for me. When I turned around, Thầy was already wheeled away. I was stunned—I had not expected Thầy could reach out that quickly. I did not try to analyze Thầy's action, I just touched his steady, powerful life force directly and realized he was not simply holding on to life for our sake. Thầy's vitality was potent, and he continued to experience life deeply until his final breath.

LIVE BEAUTIFULLY, DIE BEAUTIFULLY— TODAY

Nourishing Thầy's Great Aspirations in Myself

This meditation reflects the understanding that our actions are our continuation. It is not a practice of worship or idealization, but of embodiment. I can touch the ways my teacher's insight, compassion, and courage live on—not as memory, but as the way in which I choose to breathe, sit, and act in daily life. Even though Thầy has passed away, for me what was alive in him does not belong to the past; it remains real through what we do now. As you practice, let this be very ordinary and very human.

You are not trying to become someone else. You are allowing what has already been transmitted to take shape in your own breath, posture, understanding, and care for the world. If you wish, in place of Thầy, you can substitute the name of a person you see as a teacher, whose qualities you admire and aspire to emulate.

Breathing in, I breathe in deeply for Thầy.
Breathing out, I breathe out slowly for Thầy.
Breathing in deeply, breathing out slowly, for Thầy

Breathing in, I sit beautifully upright for Thầy.
Breathing out, I sit stably for Thầy.
Sitting upright—beautiful, stable—for Thầy

Breathing in, I see Thầy as a young monk full of energy, doing his best to bring peace to his country.
Breathing out, I am in touch with Thầy's energy and aspirations in me.
In touch with Thầy's energy and aspirations in myself

Breathing in, I am in touch with the virtue of the Great Understanding of the Bodhisattva Manjushri embodied in Thầy.
Breathing out, I nourish Thầy's Great Understanding within me, transforming my wrong views, inner knots, and habits.
Thầy's Great Understanding in me, transforming views and habits

Breathing in, I am in touch with the virtue of the Great Compassion of the Bodhisattva Avalokiteshvara embodied in Thầy.

Breathing out, I nourish Thầy's Great Compassion within me, embracing and forgiving those who cause me pain.

Thầy's Great Compassion in me, embracing and forgiving

Breathing in, I am in touch with the virtue of the Great Action of the Bodhisattva Samantabhadra embodied in Thầy.

Breathing out, I take refuge in Thầy's Great Action to build the Sangha and help others.

Thầy's Great Action in me, building the Sangha and helping others

Breathing in, I am in touch with the virtue of the Great Aspiration of the Bodhisattva Kshitigarbha embodied in Thầy.

Breathing out, I nourish Thầy's Great Aspiration within me, freeing myself from grasping and attachment.

Thầy's Great Aspiration in me, freeing me from attachment

Breathing in, I recognize that Thầy chose to remain a monk for life and opened the spiritual path for me and so many others.

Breathing out, I vow to make meaningful choices like Thầy.

Meaningful choices, opening the path for others

Breathing in, I am aware that Thầy is always in me.
Breathing out, I am aware that I am always in Thầy.
Thầy in me, I am in Thầy.

Noble Task

The Chinese app *Si le ma* (Are you dead yet?) has become one of the most downloaded apps in China, largely targeting young people. It has a single function: Users tap a button on their phones every day as virtual proof of life for their social networks. If a user fails to do so for two consecutive days, the app automatically sends an email to a chosen emergency contact. Its popularity reflects the reality of social isolation—not just in the Western world, but also in countries like China, where multiple generations often live under one roof. In today's age, the idea of living and dying alone is no longer confined to the elderly; young people face it as well. The app highlights how lonely and disconnected modern life can be. In a time when loneliness has become so widespread, the question of how we live with one another becomes one of the most important actions of our lives.

I experienced this firsthand when I was living in a college dorm. Although I served as a Resident Assistant, supposedly responsible for caring for the students on my floor, I often went days without seeing anyone. I attended classes, ate alone, spent time in the library, and returned to my dorm late at night. At times, I even thought that if I died, no one would discover my body until it had decomposed. It was a disheartening thought. Moments like these reveal how deeply human beings depend on connection. Without it, our life can begin to feel strangely invisible.

Living near and maintaining connections with family members is rare and precious. Having a supportive community of friends is equally vital. Our teacher often said building practice communities—Sanghas—is the most noble task of the twenty-first century. Why? Because the Fifth Remembrance teaches us that our actions are our true inheritance. The communities we nurture become part of the living continuation of our lives. Thầy himself was a great Sangha-builder, devoting his entire life to building and nurturing Sanghas all over the world. During the COVID-19 pandemic, many Sanghas used Zoom to practice and support each other. The Coconut Sangha, for example, met online three times a day and has continued to do so. Members from different Sanghas have reported the nourishment and support they both give and receive from their communities. When someone is sick, they pray for them and sometimes even gather to practice at their bedside. Contributing to Sangha-building is deeply meaningful. It offers us—and many others—the opportunity to cultivate genuine connection, transform and heal both individual and collective suffering, and move together toward peace and freedom.

Anger-Eating Monster

There is a story about an anger-eating monster that came to a kingdom only to be rejected and cursed by the people there.

The monster got a little bigger with every angry, hurtful word said to it. In the US and around the world, this monster is real; it is fed by division between families, communities, and nations as well as by fear, anger, hatred, and righteousness. Eventually the anger-eating monster becomes the master, dictating how we think, speak, and act.

On January 6, 2021, a mob attacked the US Capitol with the intent to prevent the formal certification of a presidential election. Videos showed senators and members of Congress trapped in the same room, hiding under tables whether they were Republicans or Democrats. At that moment, all of them just wanted to live. The monster we collectively fed had taken on a life of its own.

Perhaps some rioters believed they were acting for justice. But once triggered, their actions were no longer about ideology or allegiance but resentment, anger, and violence that took on a life of its own. Those who acted were also consumed by the monster they had fed. What was moving through them was an energy larger than that of any single person.

When a group of people act out of anger, their rational minds are no longer in control of their behavior. Dr. Dan Siegel shared a helpful brain model that we can demonstrate with our own hands. Raise your right hand with your palm facing you. Your forearm represents the spinal cord, the wrist the base of your brain, the palm the reptilian brain—the part of you that reacts instantly to perceived threat. Fold your right thumb onto the palm, and that's the limbic brain or the emotional brain. Now wrap the four fingers over the thumb, and they represent the cortical brain, like the bark of a tree. When the limbic brain interprets something as threatening—"It's a snake!"—the body immediately triggers the fight-flight-freeze response. When a group is propelled into a limbic-system fight response, the results are dire.

However, instead of instantly reacting to a stimulus, we can take a moment to stop and breathe. With just a moment of pause, the cortical brain has time to evaluate the situation more carefully and realize, "It's actually a rope, not a snake." This small pause can prevent the body from entering a cycle of repeated stress and reactivity.

I practice pausing my own fight-flight-freeze response with my own brother Sonny, who has developed a habit of making provocative political statements. Instead of getting worked up and launching a verbal counterattack, I choose to take a deep breath and remind myself, "This is my brother. I do not want to attack him for his views or beliefs." My brother has lived in Arizona for the forty years since we arrived in this country, in the company of people who hold strong views about politics. Many of his friends and associates hold the views he has naturally adopted. Had I remained in that environment, I might now hold similar views. The cortical brain has the capacity to examine situations from different angles and bring understanding and empathy. I have learned to breathe, to remain quiet, and not to fight with my brother, which would only sever our relationship. The last time I encouraged Sonny to move to California so he could live with his wife and daughter instead of commuting from Arizona on a regular basis, he told me, "If you get all the monastics to vote the way I do, I will move." I paused for a moment and replied, "I can't influence the monastics, but I will vote like you if it helps you move to California."

There is a story in *Lion's Roar* magazine titled "From Hate to Love" about a former neo-Nazi who once lived in violence.[15] It was acts of kindness that eventually helped save him. Upon reflection, he realized how much conflict had reinforced his beliefs. He had been feeding it until violence became a kind of practice and he needed it like fuel, beating other human beings to the point of hospitalization to get that hit of adrenaline. He literally used the word "practice"! He added that when you practice hate and violence, love and compassion and forgiveness and kindness—all the beautiful aspects of our human experience—become not only unfamiliar, but repulsive. "Hurt people hurt people," he said.

One day he went to McDonald's and flipped his finger—the one with the neo-Nazi sign, a swastika—at a Black cashier to frighten her. She looked at him and said, "I know you're better than that." He stormed out, but something about the way she spoke stayed with him. Slowly, he began to see his own suffering was driving his hateful behavior, and he gradually transformed.

When we respond to hatred with hatred, we feed the anger-eating monster, the very forces we wish to end. As practitioners, it is essential that we remain calm, spacious, and loving—first and foremost toward ourselves. We always begin with ourselves. We learn to pause, to breathe, to not add fuel to what is already burning. We need to remain safe to ourselves and to not wreak havoc with reactive anger and anxiety. We can bring healing to our society, but each one of us must do the work. Each one of us must re-examine our own explicit and implicit biases, recognizing that they are the source of turbulence in our world. The way out is in.

If our actions outlast us, each moment matters. Every reaction rooted in anger strengthens the pattern. Every pause rooted in awareness opens another path. Every time we respond with anger, fear, or hatred, we help the anger-eating monster grow in the generations that follow. But every time we pause, breathe, and choose understanding instead of retaliation, we nourish a different continuation. Peace, too, can be practiced. Compassion, too, can be inherited.

Suppressed Anger

Even in a spiritual community, disagreement is unavoidable. At Deer Park Monastery, monastic sisters, brothers, Dharma teachers, and elders frequently participate in many forms of meetings as part of Sangha life. We share a sincere aspiration to transform suffering and to help the world. And yet, despite that shared purpose, strong disagreements still arise among us.

Dr. Frieder, my chiropractor, is deeply spiritual and a great blessing in my life. During one of my visits, he told me, "Sister D, you have suppressed anger." I thought, "What? Me? I'm a nun. I practice mindfulness. How could I have suppressed anger?"

But he repeated it at my next visit. I asked him how he could tell. He said, "When we hold onto anger, the body reflects it. We become misaligned. One shoulder, one hip is higher than the other. There's muscle tension. The body speaks."

At first, I resisted. As I began to observe myself more closely, I realized Dr. Frieder was right. During meetings, I'd share ideas with the best intentions—more retreats, more practice days. Some would respond, "No, the community needs rest!" Then I'd feel it: breath shortening, heat rising in my chest, the impulse to walk out. Sometimes, I'd even claim I wasn't feeling well, just to skip the meeting. Over time, I've learned to anchor myself in my breath to stay present, to show up, again and again.

Thầy said harmony doesn't mean we agree on everything. It means we respect each other enough to sit and truly listen.

When I follow my breath, it begins to slow. The body relaxes. The thoughts soften. This has been one of the most important lessons: When I'm upset or frustrated, I try not to speak because words spoken from anger rarely land well. Even if I'm right, they're often met with resistance. When anger speaks, people stop listening.

No matter where we are, whenever we operate from fight, flight, or freeze, communication breaks down. If we stay with the breath throughout the day, we begin to cultivate inner harmony, which can change everything.

I remind myself often: I love and respect my community. I want to support it. To do that, I have to become a better person—not through talent or good ideas, but by tending to my own suffering. By learning to tame the anger, the frustration, the self-righteousness inside me—that is how I can truly serve others. If I were to die today, I'd want to ask myself, "Did I care for my suffering? Did I sit with it, breathe with it, and offer presence to those around me even when I was hurting?" If I can say yes, I can die in peace.

Remembering our mortality changes how we live. We don't know when our time will come, but we know that it will. So, our goal shouldn't be only to become great scientists, professors, or activists, but to become better human beings. Within each of us is the whole, and within the whole is each of us. This is the central teaching of the Avatamsaka Sutra: "The one contains the all."

When we look at the world's problems, we may feel overwhelmed. Paralyzed. Hopeless. However, if we remember we are part of the pattern and that our inner peace contributes to collective peace, our small awakenings ripple outward, and the work can feel more manageable and more tangible.

The Four Kinds of People

Caring for others is a beautiful aspiration, yet doing so can bring exhaustion, guilt, or burnout. Many of us in helping professions—doctors, nurses, therapists, counselors, teachers, parents—are trained to give but are not as well-versed in stopping, resting, or receiving. Over time, our capacity to offer genuine compassion can diminish.

The Buddha described four kinds of people. These categories can help us reflect on how we care for ourselves and for others. First, there are people who care neither for themselves nor for others. There are also those who care for others but neglect themselves, those who care for themselves but not for others, and finally, those who care for both themselves and others.[16]

It may sound surprising, but the Buddha said someone who takes care of themselves but not others is actually doing better than someone who takes care of others while neglecting themselves. When we ignore our own needs, our body eventually reminds us—through fatigue, anxiety, or illness—that something is out of balance. True compassion has roots, and those roots are nourished by rest, self-care, and stability. That might not sound immediately "Buddhist," but the point is that we must first take care of ourselves.

We all wish to offer service and leave a positive imprint on the world. However, when we take care of others while neglecting or even abusing ourselves, whatever good we do is likely to be short-lived. The noble intention we began with may turn sour or bitter. We may become quite burned out, resentful, angry, and even abusive toward those we have made the vow to love and care for, whether they are our loved ones, our patients, or our clients.

As a young doctor in training, I sometimes cried in my car before going into the hospital. I loved my patients, but there were days when I simply didn't have the strength to face more suffering. On these days, I sat in the car, cried, and waited until I could meet what awaited me. Sometimes I would go inside just to check lab results without interacting with patients—numbers felt safer than human faces. I didn't realize that I was already running on empty.

Many of us who work in healing professions don't listen to even our bodies' most basic needs. We delay using the restroom, skip meals, and push through exhaustion, telling ourselves we'll rest later. Meanwhile, the mind also accumulates fatigue. Unacknowledged feelings of frustration, resentment, fear, sadness, or grief sink below the surface until one day they overflow and we snap at a colleague or loved one, not realizing that years of unspoken tension have built up inside.

Healing cannot happen when we are divided—when the caregiver and the cared-for are seen as separate. In truth, they inter-are. Our stability helps others feel safe; our peace allows others to rest. When our energy is scattered, those we care for feel it. When we are grounded, our presence alone can bring calm.

Parents often come to me asking how to help their children. Again and again, I've seen that when parents begin to heal themselves, their children naturally begin to heal too. The most powerful gift we can offer anyone is our own freshness, steadiness, and understanding.

During the COVID-19 pandemic, nurses and doctors stood on the frontlines, risking their lives to care for patients while enduring immense pressure and stress. Many avoided close contact with their own families out of fear of spreading the virus, with some choosing to stay in hotels or isolated quarters just to protect their loved ones.

They also carried the heavy burden of grief that came with losing patients day after day and having to deliver heartbreaking news to families. One doctor, for example, called to inform a woman that her sister had just passed away. The woman replied, "I'm on my way to the funeral for my husband, my brother, and my other sister, who also died recently from COVID." Being the bearer of such devastating news, again and again, takes a deep toll on both body and mind.

Being taken for granted for risking their lives added to the burden of grief. During the first two years of the COVID-19 pandemic, millions of workers continued to be on the job providing essential services. These essential workers, including those in health care, food service, and public transportation, among others, did not receive the most basic health and safety measures to combat the spread of the coronavirus. Many essential workers died as a result. A nurse wore a T-shirt with the message on her back, "Save one, you are a hero; save a hundred, you are a nurse."

We may take for granted that people work day and night to take care of us and this world. We may forget about them when things return to normal. Many frontline workers may experience trauma and PTSD long into the future if they are not well cared for—a suffering that will affect us all. Just as Vietnam veterans were blamed, distrusted, and forgotten in ways that had lasting impacts on many families and communities, the suffering of any one person is neither private nor individual. Suffering is collective. We can each ensure that no one has to suffer alone by being able to acknowledge grief, to breathe with it, to come back to the profound reality of interbeing. Even if we are physically alone, we can reach out to help others as well as to receive support and healing.

If we care only for others, we eventually burn out. If we think selfishly only about ourselves, our heart closes and never experiences true connection and happiness. Only when we mindfully care for both ourselves and others can we touch the wholeness of love. The more we take care of our own body and mind, the more our care naturally flows to those around us. This is the art of compassionate balance: to love without losing ourselves, to serve without depletion, to remember the healer must also breathe, rest, and be healed. This balance is the most meaningful and long-lasting service we can offer ourselves and the world.

Doctors' Denial

Modern medicine has extended human life in remarkable ways. Many people now live into their eighties and nineties. The adult children who take care of these elderly may be in their sixties or seventies themselves. Yet this progress has also brought difficult questions about how we meet the final stage of life and what continuation we leave behind. When we cannot accept death, our actions—however well-intentioned—may prolong suffering rather than bring peace.

Medical advances can greatly improve quality of life. Yet they can also prolong the final stage of life through increasingly aggressive interventions, sometimes leaving people bedbound, dependent, and unable to participate in the life around them.

For example, a woman in her late eighties had severe Alzheimer's disease and many other medical conditions. Her doctor asked if her children wanted to put her on a ventilator or to allow her to pass away naturally. One daughter wanted to allow her mother to go through the natural process, but the others were determined to keep her on the respirator—they would feel guilty if they didn't do everything for their mother. Many doctors are in this dilemma as well. If they do nothing, it can feel as if they have failed their patient. Sometimes it also feels like a failure of our own ego. When we cannot accept that there may be nothing more to fix, the impulse is to intervene. This elderly woman was left on the ventilator for almost two years before she died.

Most people wish to die at home, surrounded by their loved ones. Yet the majority die in hospitals, often not from their underlying illness but instead from complications like hospital-acquired infections and medical interventions. We all have good intentions, but without the insight of interbeing and the guidance of the Five Remembrances, our efforts may reflect only our own ego—our inability to accept what is, to discern when to intervene and when to let things be, and to allow people to find peace in their final hours at home.

The Fifth Remembrance reminds us that our actions are our true inheritance. The question then becomes not only what medicine can do, but what action truly reflects wisdom and compassion. When we can see a situation clearly with "now mind" in the present moment instead of being driven only by fear, guilt, or habit, we may find the courage to accompany someone peacefully through the final stage of life rather than struggle against the natural process of dying.

When we remember that life does not simply end but continues in other forms, our relationship to death also changes. The person who is dying is not disappearing completely. Their actions, their love, their suffering, and their understanding continue in their children, their students, their communities, and in the countless lives they have touched.

Seeing Beyond Self and Other

The Diamond Sutra teaches that when we look deeply, our familiar boundaries—self versus other, human versus non-human, living beings versus non-living beings, lifespan versus immortality—begin to dissolve. These boundaries are the "four wrong views" the Buddha warned of: mistaken perceptions that keep us separate and alienated from life. We think, "This is me, that is you," or "Humans are superior to other beings." In truth, there is no separate existence. There is only interbeing—this in that, that in this, this because of that.

Once the idea of a separate self takes root, the split between self and other—as well as human versus non-human, living beings versus non-living beings, lifespan versus immortality—follows, and from it arise bias, fear, discrimination, grasping, and aversion. Individualism becomes an idol, and we forget our shared humanity. We see humans as somehow apart from or above other species and the natural world. When we fall into this illusion, the earth becomes an object of use, not a body we belong to. The Buddha taught that to see clearly is to love without boundaries. Our lifespan is the lifespan of the earth, of all living and non-living beings. To care for them is to care for ourselves.

We can see these delusions in our politics, relationships, and collective fear. When fear is triggered—through misinformation or stories of threat—it activates our most primitive instincts: fight, flight, defend, destroy. We see enemies everywhere and forget that others, too, are afraid.

The Buddha's teachings help us recognize that the "enemy" is never outside of us. It is the ignorance, greed, and fear within that divide us. Each time we return to our breath, we reclaim our capacity to see clearly. In one mindful moment, we can rise above the reactive mind and touch what the Diamond Sutra calls "suchness"—the cool, boundless presence of Nirvana that is already here.

Once, while editing one of the booklets of *Chanting from the Heart* for Deer Park Monastery, I accidentally deleted every instance of the word "Nirvana" using the "find and replace" function. Later, when I compared the files, I saw seven places where Nirvana had vanished, leaving only blank space—quiet, open, and without form. I laughed aloud. How fitting! I thought. Even the absence was teaching me. Nirvana is not a word or a place; it is this very peace that remains when nothing is grasped and nothing is lost.

When the boundary between self and other softens, our way of living changes naturally. We begin to act with more care toward one another, toward the earth, and toward the fragile web of life that sustains us. In this understanding, compassion is no longer an ideal we try to achieve. It becomes the most natural expression of seeing clearly.

Beautiful Life, Beautiful Death

I just came back to the monastery from the cremation of a dear lay friend. A few years ago, she attended a three-month Rains Retreat while already quite frail. She was always quiet and thoughtful, coming to practice with the community every Sunday despite her cancer and having to walk with a cane.

Recently, the monastic sisters visited her at home. She was bedbound, yet her face was radiant and her smile bright. She told us she had been trying all day to make an online donation to the monastery but couldn't get through, and she asked us to help her complete the bank transfer right then and there. "Make sure it's six hundred," she repeated several times. I was deeply moved that even in her final moments, she was thinking of the monastery. We sang and chanted for her—and with her. As we were leaving, I kissed her entire face, and she basked in my kisses, exclaiming, "What happiness! What happiness!"

The next day, she sent me the donation receipt. It read $600,000 USD. I emailed her immediately: "The receipt says $600,000, not $600. Is this correct? Could you please confirm?" She replied simply, "Yes. That is the amount I wish to donate to rebuild the bookshop."

When she entered hospice, I went to visit her with another sister. She lay peacefully in a morphine-induced sleep, her face marked by a deep tranquility. We spoke to her of her many beautiful virtues, sang Plum Village songs, and chanted the Beginning Anew chant. I held her hand the entire time—it was soft and warm. Her family had brought in the brown jacket she wore as a member of the lay Order of Interbeing and the set of brown clothes she always wore on Days of Mindfulness at Deer Park. At the foot of her gurney was a yellow blanket. The nurses had been instructed to change her into her practitioner's clothes and pull the yellow blanket over her body as soon as she took her last breath.

Before we left, I touched her face and noticed a difference in temperature between her facial skin and the rest of her body. Her face was noticeably cooler and slightly clammy with a faint, almost imperceptible cold sweat that I recognized from being with patients and lay friends in their final days as a sign of nearness to death. Her children told us that after we left, she smiled a single, brief smile that brought deep comfort, relief, and reassurance to her family.

She had wanted her body to be cremated within three days and without ceremony, so as not to burden her family or the monastics. In her pre-planned arrangements, no one was to be present for the cremation. In the end, however, her family changed the plan after she died so they and some monastics could attend.

When her body was brought out for us to view, the sight of a cardboard coffin took me by surprise and tears streamed down my face. Even in death she maintained her dignity, humility, and simplicity. How magnanimous she was! What a beautiful life—and a beautiful death!

The crematory operator lifted the lid of the cardboard coffin, and there she lay, her body covered with a yellow blanket and her head wrapped in a yellow scarf symbolic of the Buddha's ceremonial robe. Her face was so small and drawn I hardly recognized her. Although she had requested no makeup, a light layer of foundation and a thin touch of red lipstick had been applied, since her body had been kept in the freezer for nearly two weeks.

My elder sister chanted *"The Nectar of Compassion of Avalokiteshvara"* and sprinkled water over her entire body using a camellia flower. Then I chanted, *"This body is not me; I am not caught in this body . . ."* before we all chanted *"Namo 'Valokiteshvaraya"* in Sanskrit together.

The sisters had brought a bouquet of white roses mixed with lavender and eucalyptus branches from Deer Park Monastery, and each of us tenderly placed a rose on her body. I placed one by her face and laid the lavender and eucalyptus alongside her body. I rested my hand on her left shoulder, feeling the cold penetrate deep into my bones. In that moment, I touched the profound truth that *"this body is not me"* and realized, once again, that nothing is worth grasping or competing for in this life—in the end there is nothing we can take with us. Only a beautiful life and a beautiful death can help us transcend the mundaneness and drama of existence.

I walked with her husband to the cremation chamber, where he would press the button to close it. Everyone stood in complete silence for a few moments as the sound of the fire ignited. In that deep stillness, I initiated the Namo Avalokiteshvara Chant in Vietnamese. Our voices blended as our friend's body went into the chamber, at times rising above the roar of the flames and the hum of the machine. We were all there—for our beloved, and for one another.

No words could do justice to the experience. I offered her two adult children two calligraphies I had written that very morning: *"Beloved Mother, I see myself in you, and you are always in me."* I, too, see myself in her, and she will always be in me.

Climate Crisis: From Reactivity to Care

The climate crisis is not only an environmental crisis. It also reveals the habits of mind and heart with which we meet suffering. In times of pain, human beings often respond in familiar ways: fight, flight, or freeze. These responses are deeply human, and they shape not only our private lives but also our collective future.

Some of us fight. We fight for justice, for the environment, for peace. These are noble fights. Yet fighting is also a response to pain. It can be a way to avoid feeling the wound. Others choose flight. Flight can look like denial. In the United States, there are those who deny the climate crisis. Sometimes we lie to ourselves, and sometimes denial runs so deep that we believe the stories we tell ourselves. And then, there's freeze. When it's too much, we shut down; we numb ourselves. The body functions, but the mind checks out.

These responses can shape our entire lives. They influence how we respond to challenges—in our families, our work, our communities, and our world. The climate crisis is suffering. When we respond to it with denial, reactivity, or shutdown, we add another layer of suffering on top. Remember the first and second arrow of pain and suffering—the second arrow doesn't just double the pain; it prevents healing. Our coping mechanisms—fighting in every relationship, denying what's happening, freezing and disconnecting from ourselves and others—become that second arrow.

The other way, one deserving of our continuation, is not only in policies, protests, or ideas, but in relationships. If we love the earth as a mother, we must live that love. Recently, we held a Climate Action retreat in New Hampshire and a symposium at Harvard. Even among activists, I noticed how care was absent in the small moments—faucets left running, excessive paper towels, eyes glued to screens. If we love the earth as a mother, we care for her moment by moment, in each step, in how we breathe, how we use water, how we look at one another.

Someone shared that we now spend 95 percent of our time indoors. How can we truly protect and care for Mother Earth if we are so removed from her? How can we cultivate love for someone or something we no longer feel connected to? Our ancestors didn't call themselves climate activists, but they loved the earth. Many of them lived and died for the land. There was a deep, intimate relationship, a natural reverence and interdependence.

I grew up in Vietnam and came to the West when I was almost seventeen. My grandmother wasn't called an environmentalist, but I learned from her to live with care—perhaps because we were poor, but also because we cherished the earth. We saw the earth as a living being, a great mother, offering us everything. We conserved by instinct. We wrapped food in banana leaves, not plastic. Mindful consumption was planted in me early on.

Even now, I still wear the brown robe made for me in 2003. It was sewn in Vietnam and brought by my aunt to Plum Village. This robe is over twenty-three years old. I wear it nearly every morning for sitting meditation. It's thick, warm, and has faded with time. The pants have been turned inside out because the outside is so worn. I keep it because it's like a dear, faithful friend. This robe has been with me through so much: from when I was just three years into monastic life, through trials, healing, and transformation. It carries memory, meaning, and love.

It would be relatively easy for me to get a new robe, but no new robe would hold what this one does. That's what I mean by intimacy. When we love something, we naturally take care of it. It's not about being righteous or perfect—it's about connection. So let us deepen our connection to Mother Earth. Be outdoors more. Walk with awareness and touch the earth with each step.

After the Climate Action retreat in New Hampshire, our monastic group went to Dartmouth College for a week. On our walking meditation with students one afternoon, I asked them what they noticed. One said she heard so many sounds. Another said, "The church bell is so beautiful." One student said it felt like she stepped on grass for the first time! "Literally?" I asked. She said, "Both literally and figuratively." She had been on campus for two years, but because she was always rushing across or absorbed in her iPhone, she had never really noticed the grass beneath her feet.

If we live only in our heads—disconnected from our bodies, from each other, from the earth—then continuation is a lost cause. Suffering can be personal, it can be mental or physical, but it is also collective. The suffering of Mother Earth is tied to our way of life: wrong perceptions of separation, egocentrism, nationalism. These ideas give rise to disconnection, overconsumption, exploitation. The Buddha taught that suffering can end. How we look at suffering changes how we experience and respond to it. This is the beginning of healing. Looking deeply, we also see that the earth herself is not permanent. The Buddha taught impermanence not only in our own bodies—our skin and our hair are always changing—but in the great cycles of life as well. Earth has already experienced five mass extinctions. The one unfolding now is largely driven by human activity. Yet even without humans, impermanence would still be the nature of this planet.

Seeing this clearly does not lead to despair. It invites us to cherish what is here right now: our health, our loved ones, the forests and rivers, the fragile beauty of this living earth. When we understand impermanence deeply, care arises naturally. We act not from guilt or fear, but from love and gratitude. Reusing a piece of paper, skipping a straw, drying our clothes or our hair in the sun becomes an act of love. The mind is in the body. The body is in the mind.

Mindfulness leads to concentration. When we're present, we communicate better. We share, we listen, we collaborate—not just for ourselves, but for generations to come. Our solutions won't appear from thin air. They build on what came before, and others will build on us. That's why cooperation is so essential. As couples, families, departments, and nations, we must see our nature of interbeing. That's how real solutions are born. When care is woven into ordinary moments, the future is already being shaped.

The Human Capacity to Heal

Surely, there must be a better way to love ourselves—one that doesn't lead to war or cause suffering for ourselves and others. As a child of war, I have lived with its consequences my entire life. Animals usually kill out of hunger; humans can kill or harm each other out of greed, ignorance, or fear. Fueled by ideology, dogmatism, or fanaticism, we are capable of mass murder and widespread destruction. History shows how easily fear and rigid beliefs can turn human beings against one another. At our worst, we are like a virulent virus—a true threat to Mother Earth and all living beings.

And yet, humans can also be profoundly kind. If we learn to care for our senses, our minds, and our hearts, both individually and collectively, we can transform. There is great potential within us, not just for harm, but for deep compassion and healing.

Although I have faced many challenges, I have never regretted leaving medicine to become a nun. In fact, it's the best decision I've made in my life. I am fulfilled as a spiritual practitioner because I have been able to transform and heal the suffering within myself and my ancestors. I have cultivated the ability to love and to accept love. I often reflect on Thầy with deep gratitude. Every time I practice Touching the Earth—the act of prostrating my body on the ground in ceremony—I envision thousands of monastic practitioners in ocher ceremonial robes, all touching the earth together. Around me I see my elder sisters, younger sisters, as well as the First Venerable Nun Mahagotami—they are all my mothers. As I touch the earth with my head, I am aware that the Buddha and Thầy dwell within me. I raise my right palm upward, recognizing my father within me, and then my left palm upward, embracing my mother within me. Then, I surrender my entire body into the embrace of Mother Earth, with the following words in my mind:

I see that you are always in me
and that I am in you from time immemorial.
May I follow your good example
and live every moment with true peace and joy.

When we touch the earth in this way, we touch our deepest nature—our capacity to transform suffering into understanding and compassion. The same human mind that can create suffering also has the capacity to awaken, to love, and to care for the earth and for one another. From this understanding, our actions begin to change.

LIVE BEAUTIFULLY, DIE BEAUTIFULLY— TODAY

Touching the Earth

When we touch the earth, we touch the vast stream of life that has carried us until now and will continue long after this body is gone. This is a practice of returning to the very earth of our being. Each earth touching is a way of releasing what no longer serves and reaffirming the direction of our life. Each rising is an affirmation that we can begin again.

Before beginning this practice, take a moment to arrive fully in your body. Allow your breath to settle, and feel your weight being supported by the earth beneath you.

Bring your palms together in front of your chest, like a lotus bud. When you are ready to touch the earth, raise your joined palms to your forehead, then slowly lower them past your heart. As your body descends toward the ground, gently open your arms like wings.

When your body comes to rest on the earth in a child's pose, turn your palms upward in a gesture of openness and receptivity. Follow your breathing, relax your entire body, and allow yourself to rest deeply as you contemplate.

Breathing in, I feel my body supported by the earth.
Breathing out, I release tension and return to this moment.

Breathing in, I touch the countless conditions—seen and unseen—that have allowed me to be here.
Breathing out, I offer my gratitude to all who have made my life possible.

Breathing in, I touch my ancestors—blood, spiritual, animal, and land—within every cell of my body.
Breathing out, I bow to their joys, their sorrows, and their unfinished dreams.

Breathing in, I am aware that my thoughts, words, and actions are my true continuation.
Breathing out, I plant seeds of understanding, compassion, and courage.

Breathing in, I see that I am continued through those I love, by those I teach, and by those whose lives I touch unknowingly.

Breathing out, I offer them my best—my clarity, my presence, my deep aspiration.

Breathing in, I release the idea of a separate self.

Breathing out, I rest in the great river of interbeing.

Breathing in, I touch the vastness of life moving through me.

Breathing out, I bow to this moment with humility and awe.

This is the practice of continuation offered with our whole body, our whole being. Each time we touch the earth, we return to what is most true. We remember, as the Buddha taught, that our actions are our only true belongings—the ground of our continuation.

May each breath, each step, each thought be worthy of the world we will one day leave behind. May the quality of our actions today become the refuge and the continuation we offer to all beings.

AFTERWORD

The Path Continues

We have walked together through the Five Remembrances: aging, illness, death, separation from all we love, and the truth that our actions are our continuation. These reflections are not meant to burden the heart. They are invitations to wake up and live with more joy and appreciation.

When we remember that we will grow old, we learn to care more gently for the body that we have now. When we remember that illness can arise at any time, we learn not to take health for granted. When we remember that death is certain, we begin to value each breath more deeply. When we remember that everyone and everything we love will change and one day be separated from us, we learn to love without clinging. And when we remember that our actions are our true inheritance, we begin to live with greater mindfulness and care.

These truths are not far away. They are already present here, in this moment.

Perhaps, as you read these pages, you recognized parts of your own story—moments of fear, moments of tenderness, moments when life revealed its fragility and beauty at the same time. If so, you are not alone. Every human being walks this path. We are companions in being born, loving, losing, and beginning again.

The practice is not something separate from daily life. It is found in the most ordinary moments. When you take a step and feel the earth supporting you; when you pause before speaking and choose words that bring understanding rather than harm; when you sit quietly beside someone who is suffering; when you smile at a child, a stranger, or the morning light—each of these small acts is already part of your continuation.

Aging will continue. Illness will come and go. Death will one day arrive. These truths cannot be avoided. But they do not have to make us afraid. When we learn to live with awareness of impermanence, life becomes more vivid, more precious, more real. We discover that even in the presence of loss, there is still beauty. Even in uncertainty, there is still the possibility of love. We do not need to control life, only to meet it with an open heart.

At any moment, we can return to the breath. Breathing in, we know we are alive. Breathing out, we smile to this moment. Perhaps right now you can pause. Feel the body sitting or standing where you are. Feel the breath moving quietly in and out. Notice that this moment is already enough. You do not need to wait for some future time to begin living beautifully. The opportunity is in this breath, in this step, in this small act of kindness. Each day we can choose to live in a way that brings more understanding, more compassion, and more peace into the world. Even imperfectly, our life becomes a gift to those around us.

When the time comes for our last breath, we may discover there is nothing to regret and nothing to fear. We have lived fully human lives and gained authentic insights, loving and caring for ourselves, other fellow beings, and Mother Earth as soulmates. Our life's journey has indeed been a quiet revolution. We have done our best to transform our habits and ease the suffering within ourselves and in the world. No material wealth or titles can be carried with us in that final moment, yet our legacy lives on in the hearts of those we love and all those we have touched. And that is enough.

Breathing in, I live beautifully today.

Breathing out, I touch the wonder of being alive.

May this understanding of the Five Remembrances support us on our path. May we walk gently on this earth, cherishing the people we meet and the moments that make up our life.

Ceremonies and Practices

These ceremonies come from a living monastic tradition, where they are practiced within the rhythm and collective energy of the monastic community. Most readers, however, will be engaging them in homes, hospitals, funeral chapels, or community spaces. Please feel free to adapt the language, length, and structure to fit your own context, beliefs, and level of experience. If you have practiced at a monastery before, you may draw from that embodied memory. If not, you might consider consulting a trusted teacher, practitioner, or community member to support you in shaping a form that feels steady and authentic. What matters most is not perfect form, but sincerity, presence, and love.

Ceremony to Support the Sick and the Deceased

This ceremony is offered for those who would like a more formal way to pray, sit, and gather for someone who is ill or who has died. In the monastery, these chants are practiced within a Buddhist tradition, but at heart they are expressions of love, presence, and remembrance. You can find this and other supportive ceremonies in the Plum Village book of ceremonies and practices, *Chanting from the Heart*.[17]

You do not need to be Buddhist to use this ceremony. You are welcome to adapt the language so it reflects your own beliefs and understanding. You may follow the entire sequence, or simply choose one or two elements that feel supportive. What matters most is not the form itself, but the intention behind it: to sit together, to breathe, to remember, and to offer love.

If some of the words feel unfamiliar, you can let them wash over you like poetry. Take what resonates. Leave what does not. Allow the ceremony to become something living and personal in your own home or community.

Prepare a quiet, sacred space. Light candles in mindfulness and put flowers around the person. Whether the sick or deceased is at home or in the hospital, conscious or unconscious, those present may gather around the person for this ceremony.

Start with a few minutes of silent sitting meditation. If it feels meaningful to you, you may light incense. Watching it burn and transform into fragrance can help us reflect on change, ephemerality, and the invisible threads that connect us beyond birth and death. The introductory remarks and chants may be read aloud by one person, or shared in turns if family members or friends are joining you.

If you have a Buddhist bell, you may like to invite a bell sound at points in the ceremony marked [Bell].

At the end of the ceremony, family members and friends may practice hugging meditation and share fond memories, positive attributes, and heartfelt appreciation for your loved one.

1. Sitting Meditation (5–10 minutes)
2. Incense offering
3. Introductory Words
4. Chanting

   The Insight that Brings Us to the Other Shore

   Contemplation on No-Coming and No-Going

   Beginning Anew

   Taking Refuge

   Sharing the Merit
5. Hugging Meditation and personal sharing

Introductory Words

Today, the community has gathered to honor the beautiful life and transition of our beloved (mother, father, grandparent, child, friend), ______________________, born on ______________________, and who transitioned on ______________________ in ______________________, at the age of ______________________.

Relatives and friends are all here to take part in this ceremony. Please remember that our loved one—whether still living or having left this life—is present in all of us here. Their life, and the lives of their ancestors, continue in each of us.

According to the teachings of the Buddha, the peace and joy of the children and grandchildren are the peace and joy of the parents, grandparents, and all ancestors.

We invite the community to be fully present with calm and spacious minds. Let us be aware of our breathing and of the precious presence of everyone gathered here today. Together, may we send our love and support to our beloved, and to one another, during these profound moments of transformation and healing.

Opening Verse

Namo Tassa Bhagavato Arahato Samma Sambuddhassa
(repeat 3 times) [Bell]

The Dharma is deep and lovely.

We now have a chance to see, study, and practice it.

We vow to realize its true meaning. [Bell]

The Insight That Brings Us to the Other Shore

Avalokiteshvara

while practicing deeply with

the Insight that Brings Us to the Other Shore,

suddenly discovered that

all of the five Skandhas are equally empty,

and with this realization

he overcame all Ill-being. [Bell]

"Listen Sariputra,

this Body itself is Emptiness

and Emptiness itself is this Body.
This Body is not other than Emptiness
and Emptiness is not other than this Body.
The same is true of Feelings,
Perceptions, Mental Formations,
and Consciousness. [Bell]

"Listen Sariputra,
all phenomena bear the mark of Emptiness:
their true nature is the nature of
no Birth no Death,
no Being no Non-being,
no Defilement no Purity,
no Increasing no Decreasing.
That is why in Emptiness,
Body, Feelings, Perceptions,
Mental Formations and Consciousness
are not separate self-entities.
The Eighteen Realms of Phenomena
which are the six Sense Organs,
the six Sense Objects,
and the six Consciousnesses
are also not separate self-entities.
The Twelve Links of Interdependent Arising
and their Extinction
are also not separate self-entities.

Ill-being, the Causes of Ill-being,
the End of Ill-being, the Path,
insight and attainment,
are also not separate self-entities.
Whoever can see this
no longer needs anything to attain. [Bell]

Bodhisattvas who practice
the Insight that Brings Us to the Other Shore
see no more obstacles in their mind,
and because there
are no more obstacles in their mind,
they can overcome all fear,
destroy all wrong perceptions
and realize Perfect Nirvana. [Bell]

All Buddhas in the past, present and future
by practicing
the Insight that Brings Us to the Other Shore
are all capable of attaining
Authentic and Perfect Enlightenment.
Therefore, Sariputra,
it should be known that
the Insight that Brings Us to the Other Shore
is a Great Mantra,
the most illuminating mantra,

the highest mantra,

a mantra beyond compare,

the True Wisdom that has the power

to put an end to all kinds of suffering. [Bell]

Therefore, let us proclaim

a mantra to praise

the Insight that Brings Us to the Other Shore:

Gate, gate, pāragate, pārasaṃgate, bodhi svāhā!
(repeat 3 times) [Bell x2]

Contemplation on No-Coming and No-Going

This body is not me.

I am not limited by this body. I am life without boundaries.

I have never been born, and I have never died.

Look at the ocean and the sky filled with stars,

manifestations from my wondrous True Mind.

Since before time, I have been free.

Birth and death are only doors through which we pass,

sacred thresholds on our journey.

Birth and death are a game of hide-and-seek.

So laugh with me, hold my hand,

let us say goodbye,

say goodbye, to meet again soon.

We meet today.

We will meet again tomorrow.

We will meet at the source every moment.

We meet each other in all forms of life. [Bell]

Beginning Anew

With great respect, we turn towards the Conqueror of Afflictions,

offering heartfelt words of repentance.

We have lived in forgetfulness for so long.

As we have not had the opportunity to encounter the Dharma,

our habit energies have led us into suffering.

We have made many mistakes out of unskillfulness.

We have been blinded by our askew perceptions for a long time.

Our heart's garden is sown with attachment, hatred, and pride.

In us are seeds of killing, stealing, sexual misconduct, and lies.

Our everyday deeds and words can do damage.

All of these unskillful actions are obstacles to our peace and joy.

May we begin anew. [Bell]

We see that we have been thoughtless,

straying from the path of mindfulness.

We have stored up afflictions and ignorance,

which brought about much sorrow and resentment.

There have been times we are weary of life, full of worries and anxiety.

With no understanding of others,

we become angry and resentful.

First we try to reason, and then we blame.

Every day the suffering increases, making the rift greater.

There are days that we do not want to speak or to even look at each other,

thereby creating longstanding internal formations.

Now we turn to the Three Jewels.

Sincerely recognizing our mistakes, we bow our heads. [Bell]

We know so well that in our consciousness

are buried all the wholesome seeds;

seeds of love and understanding, and seeds of peace and joy.

But because we do not know how to water them,

the wholesome seeds do not sprout in abundance.

We continue to allow sorrow to overwhelm us until there is no light in our lives.

When we chase after a distant happiness,

life becomes but a shadow of reality.

Our mind is occupied by the past or worried about the future.

We cannot let go of our anger,

and we consider of no value the precious gifts of life

that are already in our hands,

thereby trampling on real happiness.
As month follows month, we are sinking in sorrow.
So now in the precious presence of the Buddha,
fragrant with sandalwood incense,
we recognize our errors and begin anew. [Bell]

With all our hearts we go for refuge,
turning to the Buddhas in the Ten Directions
and all of the Bodhisattvas, noble disciples, and self-achieved Buddhas.
Sincerely we recognize our misdeeds and our wrong judgments.
Please pour the clear nectar
onto the roots of our afflictions to extinguish them.
Please bring the raft of the true teachings
to carry us over the ocean of sorrow.
We vow to live an awakened life,
to learn the teachings authentically transmitted,
and to practice smiling and mindful breathing.
Diligently, we cultivate mindfulness in every moment. [Bell]

We come back to the wonderful present
to plant our heart's garden with good seeds,
and to strengthen our understanding and love.
We vow to train ourselves in meditation,
practicing to look and understand deeply

to see the true nature of all phenomena,

and so to be free of the bonds of birth and death.

We learn to speak lovingly, to be affectionate,

taking care of others whether it is early morning or late afternoon,

bringing the source of joy to many places,

helping to alleviate sorrows,

and repaying the deep gratitude

to the kindness of parents, teachers, and friends.

With deep faith we light up the incense of our heart.

We ask the Lord of Compassion to be our protector

on the wonderful path of practice.

We vow to practice diligently,

realizing the highest attainment of the path. [Bell x2]

The Three Refuges

I take refuge in the Buddha, the one who shows me the way in this life.

I take refuge in the Dharma, the way of understanding and of love.

I take refuge in the Sangha, the community that lives in harmony and awareness. [Bell]

Dwelling in the refuge of Buddha, I clearly see the path of light and beauty in the world.

Dwelling in the refuge of Dharma, I learn to open many doors on the path of transformation.

Dwelling in the refuge of Sangha, shining light that supports me, keeping my practice free of obstruction. [Bell]

Taking refuge in the Buddha in myself, I aspire to help all people recognize their own awakened nature, realizing the Mind of Love.

Taking refuge in the Dharma in myself, I aspire to help all people fully master the ways of practice, and walk together on the path of liberation.

Taking refuge in the Sangha in myself, I aspire to help all people build Fourfold communities, to embrace all beings and support their transformation. [Bell x2]

Sharing the Merit

Reciting the sutras, practicing the way of awareness,

gives rise to benefits without limit.

We vow to share the fruit with all beings.

We vow to offer tribute to parents, teachers, friends, and numerous beings who give guidance and support along the path. [Bell x3]

Hugging Meditation

Dear friends and family, throughout this ceremony you have been reminded that the peace and joy you experience now are the peace and joy of your beloved. To express your love and gratitude you're invited to come together [in front of the altar if there is one], turn toward one another, and simply look into each other's eyes, letting love, acceptance, and forgiveness be there.

If your beloved could speak to you now, their deepest wish would likely be that each of you live your life beautifully and lovingly. You might take a quiet moment to promise that you will continue to love and care for one another, forgiving mistakes—past and future—as best you can. As you embrace each other, feel how alive and precious this person is to you. Also touch the presence of your beloved alive in you and in between you. Take three slow breaths together, fully aware of each inhale and each exhale. How wonderful it is that you are still alive and that you still have each other!

Let us all remain established in mindfulness, offering our spiritual support to the relatives and friends of the deceased as they practice hugging meditation.

Tending to an Altar

After a funeral, it is customary for the family to establish or update a home altar for the deceased. This altar typically includes a photo of the loved one, an incense urn, fresh flowers, and possibly some fruits. If the family already has a collective ancestral altar, the new photograph may be placed beside those of earlier generations—parents, grandparents, and so on.

Family members may light incense at any time, especially in moments when they wish to connect with the departed. In the first week after the passing, it is common to prepare a favorite dish of the deceased and offer it at the altar each day.

Special ceremonies are held weekly for seven weeks, beginning on the seventh day after death and continuing through the forty-ninth day. On these days, families may place offerings of food, fruits, flowers, and incense on the altar. Loved ones gather to send their heartfelt energy, prayers, and expressions of love and gratitude to the deceased. After the ceremony, the food offered may be shared in a communal meal, symbolizing continued connection and remembrance.

Larger ceremonies are also held on the one-hundredth day, the first anniversary, and the second anniversary of the passing. After that, families typically hold an annual memorial gathering on the anniversary date. On these occasions, loved ones come together to cook, perform a ceremony, and share a meal in remembrance. Family members may take turns to share loving, joyful memories of the deceased. We can share how we see our beloved in one another, how we recognize and continue them in our lives.

The altar remains a living part of the household, a place to share family news such as the birth of a child, a graduation, a wedding, or restored health with those who have passed. These joyful updates can be shared anytime, aloud or silently.

Ultimately, these practices help us carry the memory and spirit of the deceased within our hearts and daily lives. They are expressions of love and continuity, offering comfort, connection, and healing. At the same time, they serve as antidotes to denial, grief, and isolation, reminding us that no one truly disappears when they are held in memory and love.

Our love, our peace, and our shared joy are the most real and beautiful continuation of our beloved.

NOTES

1 Bhikkhu Bodhi, *The Connected Discourses of the Buddha: A Translation of the Samyutta Nikaya (Wisdom Publications, 2003),* SN 22.28.

2 Thich Nhat Hanh, "Discourse on Youth and Happiness," in *Chanting from the Heart, Volume 1: Buddhist Sutras and Chants for Recitation* (Parallax Press, 2023), 59.

3 Nhat Hanh, "Discourse on Youth and Happiness."

4 James Doty, *Mind Magic: The Neuroscience of Manifestation and How It Changes Everything* (Yellow Kite, 2024).

5 Thich Nhat Hanh, "The Discourse on the Full Awareness of Breathing" and "The Discourse on the Four Establishments of Mindfulness," in *Chanting from the Heart, Volume 1.*

6 Norman Doidge, *The Brain That Changes Itself: Stories of Personal Triumph from the Frontiers of Brain Science* (Penguin Life, 2007).

7 Markham Held, "Depression and Suicide Rates Are Rising Sharply in Young Americans, New Report Says. This May Be One Reason Why," *Time*, March 14, 2019. *https://time.com/collections/davos-2020-mental-health/5550803/depression-suicide-rates-youth/.*

8 Nhat Hanh, "Discourse on Youth and Happiness."

9 Nhat Hanh, "Discourse on Youth and Happiness."

10 Thich Nhat Hanh, "Turning to the Tathagata," in *Chanting from the Heart, Volume 1.*

11 Nyanponika Thera and Helmuth Hecker, *Great Disciples of the Buddha: Their Lives, Their Works, Their Legacy*, ed. Bhikku Bodhi (Wisdom Publications, 1997).

12 "The Insight That Brings Us to the Other Shore," Thich Nhat Hanh's translation of the Heart Sutra in English, can be found on the Plum Village website, along with an audio recording and sheet music: *https://plumvillage.org/library/sutras/the-heart-sutra*. Accessed April 28, 2026.

13 "Epitaph of Jalaluddin Rumi," in *The Way of the Sufi*, ed. Idries Shah (Octagon Press, 2004), TK.

14 The text of the Five Mindfulness Trainings can be found on the Plum Village website: *https://plumvillage.org/mindfulness/the-5-mindfulness-trainings*. Accessed April 28, 2026.

15 Lindsay Kyte, "An Ex-Neo-Nazi's Journey to Buddhism," *Lion's Roar*, May 16, 2018, TK–TK.

16 Bhikkhu Bodhi, "The Book of Fours," in *The Numerical Discourses of the Buddha: An Anthology of Suttas from the Anguttara Nikaya* (Yale University Press, 2010), AN 4.95.

ACKNOWLEDGMENTS

I would like to express my deepest gratitude to my beloved teacher, Zen Master Thich Nhat Hanh. You have shown me the way back into myself to find light and beauty. I am because you are.

Thank you to my beloved grandmother, who showed me love and guided me to the spiritual path.

To my mother and father, who gave me a chance in this life and transmitted to me many wonderful virtues.

To my dear brother Sonny, Trang, and Sunee, for being my family and giving me deep joy and hope.

To my monastic brothers and sisters, for supporting me on the path and allowing me time and space to heal and to flower.

To my professors and colleagues at UCSF and Martinez. Deep gratitude to Dr. Fish for keeping my letters all these years, looking for me, and writing me a loving foreword. I am also grateful for Larry Kasanoff and his brother, Bruce, for their kind support.

To all the aunties, uncles, young people, and lay friends who have loved me and supported me as your own family member.

To dearest Cyrus Maher, and to Hisae Matsuda, Katie Eberle, and Miranda Perrone of Parallax Press, for believing in me and helping to make this book a reality. Miranda worked tirelessly as my editor and collaborator. So much of her love, wisdom, and courage shine through in this book. You made this topic of living and dying your own, deeply and personally, and I cherish your presence.

To all the friends who entrusted their life stories to me. You help deepen my own understanding, compassion, and practice.

To my dear readers, for your bravery and your beauty. May you find your own voices and aspirations in reading this book. May you make a commitment to live with more beauty and freedom.

ABOUT THE AUTHOR

PHOTO BY RON FORSTER

Sister Dang Nghiem is a disciple of the revered Zen Master Thich Nhat Hanh. After losing her mother at the age of twelve, she moved to the United States with her brother at the age of seventeen, where she learned English and went on to earn a medical degree from the University of California, San Francisco. After suffering further tragedy and the loss of her partner, she quit her practice as a doctor to travel to Plum Village monastery in France, founded by Zen Master Thich Nhat Hanh, where she ordained as a nun in 2000. Her writing draws on her unique experiences as a physician, a nun, and an individual navigating diverse worlds. She is the author of four other books: a memoir, *Healing: A Woman's Journey from Doctor to Nun* (2010); *Mindfulness as Medicine: A Story of Healing and Spirit* (2015); *Flowers in the Dark: Reclaiming Your Power to Heal from Trauma with Mindfulness* (2021); and a collection of poems, *The River in Me: Verses of Transformation* (2024).

Monastics and visitors practice the art of mindful living in the tradition of Thich Nhat Hanh at our mindfulness practice centers around the world. To reach any of these communities, or for information about how individuals, couples, and families can join in a retreat, please contact:

PLUM VILLAGE
24240 Thénac, France
plumvillage.org

LA MAISON DE L'INSPIR
77510 Villeneuve-sur-Bellot, France
maisondelinspir.org

HEALING SPRING MONASTERY
77510 Verdelot, France
healingspringmonastery.org

MAGNOLIA GROVE MONASTERY
Batesville, MS 38606, USA
magnoliagrovemonastery.org

BLUE CLIFF MONASTERY
Pine Bush, NY 12566, USA
bluecliffmonastery.org

DEER PARK MONASTERY
Escondido, CA 92026, USA
deerparkmonastery.org

EUROPEAN INSTITUTE OF APPLIED BUDDHISM
D-51545 Waldbröl, Germany
eiab.eu

THAILAND PLUM VILLAGE
Nakhon Ratchasima
30130 Thailand
thaiplumvillage.org

ASIAN INSTITUTE OF APPLIED BUDDHISM
Lantau Island, Hong Kong
pvfhk.org

STREAM ENTERING MONASTERY
Porcupine Ridge, Victoria 3461 Australia
nhapluu.org

MOUNTAIN SPRING MONASTERY
Bilpin, NSW 2758, Australia
mountainspringmonastery.org

For more information visit: *plumvillage.org*
To find an online sangha visit: *plumline.org*
For more resources, try the Plum Village app: *plumvillage.app*
Social media: *@thichnhathanh @plumvillagefrance*

THICH NHAT HANH FOUNDATION

planting seeds of Compassion

THE THICH NHAT HANH FOUNDATION works to continue the mindful teachings and practices of Zen Master Thich Nhat Hanh in order to foster peace and transform suffering in all people, animals, plants, and our planet. Through donations to the Foundation, thousands of generous supporters ensure the continuation of Thich Nhat Hanh's vision and help care for practice centers and monastics around the world. Your gifts help bring transformative practices to people who otherwise could not access them and support local mindfulness initiatives that ease suffering and cultivate joy.

By becoming a supporter, you join thousands of others committed to learning about, embodying, and sharing the life-changing practices of mindfulness, loving speech, deep listening, and compassion for oneself, each other, and the world.

For more information on how you can help spread Thich Nhat Hanh's teachings and practices globally, and to subscribe to our newsletters offering teachings, news, and information about retreats, please visit tnhf.org.